Discerning the Word

The Bible and Homosexuality in Anglican Debate

Paul Gibson

Anglican Book Centre
Toronto, Canada

Published
2000 by
Anglican Book Centre
600 Jarvis Street
Toronto, Ontario
M4Y 2J6

Canadian Cataloguing in Publication Data
Gibson, Paul, 1932-
   Discerning the word: the Bible and homosexuality in Anglican debate

ISBN 1-55126-320-3

1. Homosexuality — Religious aspects — Anglican Communion. 2. Anglican Communion — Doctrines. 3. Lambeth Conference (1998: Canterbury, England). I. Title.

BR115.H6G52 2000   261.8'35766'08823   C00-931891-7

Discerning the Word

Contents

For Patrick and Rob,
and Oriole and Sherry

Preface

FOR ABOUT 130 years the bishops of the Anglican Communion have gathered at roughly ten-year intervals to discuss the affairs of their church and the challenges of the world. Originally they met at Lambeth Palace, the official residence of the Archbishop of Canterbury, and their meetings have consequently been known as the Lambeth Conferences. Recent conferences, however, have been held in the residences and other facilities of the University of Kent in Canterbury, and the bishops have gone to Lambeth only for formal and official events. But the name has stuck.

The Lambeth Conferences do not pretend to be in the same league as the great councils of the church that hammered out the terms of Christian orthodoxy in the fourth and fifth centuries. They do not even claim the same authority as councils convoked in succeeding centuries. They are not like the councils of the Roman Catholic Church, which have a certain legislative capacity. (The first Vatican Council in 1871 declared the Pope to be infallible when he rules officially, and the second Vatican Council, which met in the 1960s, radically changed the direction of the Roman Catholic Church in worship, ecumenical relationships, and other matters.) The Lambeth Conferences are just what their name implies: an opportunity for the bishops of the Communion to share problems and insights and to propose to one another those directions of policy that are most likely to maintain the integrity and unity of the Anglican world.

The decisions of the Lambeth Conferences are advisory, not prescriptive. They are also advisory for the moment in which they are made, not necessarily forever. The Lambeth Conferences have proposed quite different positions on the question of the legitimacy of contraception, for instance, reflecting different stages in the church's development of thought on the matter.[1] However, this advisory and provisional role of the Lambeth Conferences does not mean that they have no authority at all. On the contrary, they have a right to be taken very seriously in the church's subsequent conversations and deliberations. If they do not have the authority of a law or a veto, they have at least the authority of a corporate senior voice, which must be respected even if it is not obeyed.

It became clear long before the 1998 Lambeth Conference that the status of homosexuals in the church would be a major area of discussion. The subject has many dimensions, but two of the presenting issues are the possibility of blessing the commitment of couples of the same sex to live in a covenant relationship parallel to Christian marriage, and the acceptance of people in such relationships as ordained ministers of the church.

Clearly there is pressure in a number of provinces of the Communion to change accepted standards of church discipline in these and other areas affecting the lives of homosexual Christians. This should not be entirely surprising because the church's

---

1   Compare Resolution 41 of 1908, Resolution 68 of 1920, and Resolution 15 of 1930.

traditional position has not always been matched in actual practice. Discreet behaviour outside of accepted norms has often been unquestioned and unchallenged, and toleration has provided a somewhat negative but nevertheless real form of blessing—for ordained as well as lay members of the church. More than twenty years ago a very conservative archbishop told me that it was his policy to tell clergy he knew to be homosexual that he did not expect any man (sic) to be celibate and that he required them only to engage in sexual relationships outside the parish and to stay away from children. Unfortunately, this well-intentioned approach was based on a number of frightening misconceptions, including the notions that homosexual relationships are usually casual or desperate adventures based on the relief of sexual need rather than expressions of mutually supportive love, and that homosexual people are more open to the perversion of paedophilia than others. Many people now believe that toleration based on a mixture of benign ignorance, rampant hypocrisy, and aloof distaste will not do.

Other forces, some unexpected, have come into play. Before the AIDS plague began in the 1980s, it was possible for many people in Western society to pretend they were not really familiar with homosexuality, even if deep down they knew otherwise. Once people began dying in droves of a disease that was, in the West, most often transmitted in the male homosexual community (the situation is otherwise in Africa) the sexual orientation of a significant section of the population could no longer be politely ignored. The sheer numbers of the victims of AIDS, and the disease's impact on family and friendship networks throughout society, eventually gave homosexuality a recognizable human face. People who had been collectivized as "different" or "queer" (or worse) became identifiable human beings with a claim on compassion in the person of the boy next door or a colleague at work or a spouse's cousin.

In the meantime, the very basis of sexual morality was changing in Western society. What had been largely a system of taboos was (especially in the 1960s) being changed into an area for individual decision-making. The effects of this transformation were very mixed—a blend of greater freedom with greater opportunity for exploitation. However, there is little doubt that attitudes to sexual morality altered substantially in the second half of the twentieth century, even among those whose behaviour remained generally consistent with traditional codes of morality.

A major factor in this change in attitude was the invention of oral contraceptives for women. Before "the pill" traditional morality had been constantly reinforced by the fear of pregnancy—a fear only partly alleviated by the availability of mechanical forms of contraception[2] and the social stigmas attached to the three evils of unmarried motherhood, so-called "illegitimacy," and hasty marriages followed by short pregnancies. The dark alternative of abortion was scarcely mentioned. After the arrival of the pill, people felt much more free to make moral decisions on the basis of what they perceived to be responsible behaviour rather than religious and social constraint. Gradually the practice of "living together" became increasingly common and must today be regarded as one of the accepted lifestyles in Western society, among church people as well as in secular contexts. The single-parent mother is now a culturally

---

2   It is worth remembering that as recently as 1916 Margaret Sanger served thirty days in the workhouse for running a birth control clinic. The clinic was branded a "public nuisance."

accepted and generally approved reality, whether outside of marriage or after a divorce. Rigid and traditional morality has been seen in retrospect by many to have been the victim of so many half-cloaked exceptions that it appeared tarnished with the stain of hypocrisy in comparison to thoughtful and responsible decision-making.

This more liberal and situational[3] approach was bound to create an environment in which many heterosexual people adopted a more tolerant attitude to the relationships of homosexuals around them, and in which homosexual people increasingly laid claim to that toleration as an affirmation of their human dignity. In North America a number of agencies have been working for gay and lesbian rights since the 1970s. Where toleration was missing, homosexual people increasingly put themselves and their community in the public spotlight through affirmations of their own self-worth and expressions of pride in being as they were. This latter move was accelerated and reinforced in some places by the callous and brutal behaviour of law enforcement agencies who raided sites known as homosexual gathering places to humiliate and harass the occupants.[4] Today the annual Gay Pride parades in a number of

---

3   "Situational ethics" is the belief that ethical imperatives are found in the situations in which moral questions arise, in the light of certain overarching principles like, "You shall love your neighbour as yourself," and do not inhere in rigid and unvarying rules with an independent existence outside of the context, from which they may be applied to particular circumstances. For an interesting presentation of the subject, see Joseph Fletcher, *Situation Ethics: The New Morality*, The Westminster Press, Philadelphia, 1966.

4   There was a notable riot in New York City after a police raid on a gay bar in 1969, which led to the organization of the first "Gay Pride" celebrations. Toronto police made a similar raid on bathhouses a few years later.

North American cities attract hundreds of thousands of partici-
pants, including heterosexual parents and friends of lesbians and
gays who wish to foster acceptance of the homosexual community and bring prejudice against gay and lesbian people to an
end. Some church groups play conspicuous roles in these events.

I have sketched these events (and it is only a sketch) largely
from a neutral or even secular point of view, but noting that
they were not without impact on church communities. Of
course, these issues have also been deeply divisive for Christians in Western cultures, including Anglicans, and still are.
However, in the context of this historical framework it is hardly
surprising that homosexual Christians—and there are many of
them—ask their churches to treat them with respect and dignity. They do not ask for approval of homosexual
licentiousness and promiscuity any more than heterosexual
Christians ask for approval of heterosexual debauchery. They
ask the church to offer public prayers of blessing on their commitment to live together in steadfast and responsible love and
to support and encourage them. They ask that those who have
made such commitments not be barred from the exercise of
ministry.

All of this—cultural and social change, the openness of some
Anglicans to theological revision and the disagreement of others, the settled positions of people in non-Western cultures that
have not experienced the same kind of change in either church
or society, and the aspirations of devout Anglican homosexuals
for full and unequivocal acceptance—was part of the baggage
that arrived for the consideration of the bishops at the 1998
Lambeth Conference.

It was a privilege for me to be at the 1998 Lambeth Conference as a member of supporting staff. I was not, however, present
at any of the deliberations of the section of the Conference

charged with responsibility for dealing with issues of sexuality, and my knowledge of the work of the Conference on this subject was *not* based on access to privileged data. In reflecting on the decisions of the Conference I will make use only of information that would have been available to any accredited visitor or member of the press because that is the only information I have. I ask only not to be disqualified from participation in the ongoing discussion (a discussion assumed by one of the Conference resolutions, as will be seen) because of my proximity to the events. Of course, my opinions are mine alone and must not be attributed to the various bodies in the Communion, provincial, international, voluntary, and official, with which I have been associated. It should not be assumed that anyone agrees with me unless and until they state publicly that they have come to the same conclusions.

It became apparent early in the Conference that the divisions of opinion and judgement were deeper and more complicated than might at first have been assumed. There were not only different ways of arguing to a conclusion, there were radically different ways of seeing and understanding the subject and the elements of Christian tradition on which a response might be based. During the early days of the Conference a small bell kept ringing in my mind, reminding me of a tool or model I had once known that had been designed to illuminate these different, culturally conditioned perspectives of understanding. Eventually I remembered my source, and I have applied it as best I can in the first chapter below. I have tried to use it to analyze the nature of our divisions, not only in Western society but globally, and to understand how it is that, as one moves from the relatively simple disagreements of Western culture into a multicultural scene, the discussion becomes increasingly complicated and puzzling.

However, if I am concerned about the integrity of the church's response to committed and faithful homosexual people, I am even *more* concerned about what the Lambeth Conference said about the place of Scripture in the Anglican Communion as the basis for its position on issues of homosexuality. I blush to say I am *more* concerned, for how can one be more concerned with a point of theology than with the pastoral care of people? However, the Lambeth Conference left the issue of sexuality relatively if not entirely unchanged from the discipline we have received from the past: homosexual people are not worse off in the church than they were before, although they may not be better off. But on the issue of Scripture the Lambeth Conference moved, I believe, into new territory, distancing itself from the cautious, liberal, and temperate position expressed in Article VI[5] of the Thirty-nine Articles of Religion (which together constitute one of the charter documents of sixteenth-century Anglicanism) and the traditional Anglican ordinals. It is my belief that wholesale adoption of the Lambeth Conference's position on Scripture would leave us very much worse off than before, and in ways that would eventually affect the nature of the pastoral care we offer. How we understand, use, and present the Bible will eventually affect its credibility and reception, and consequently the capacity of people to find in it the living record of the salvation of the people of God, which has power to address and confront the alienation that people suffer in every generation. I hope to show that this is no small matter.

Further, I feel I owe my lesbian and gay friends an explanation, if not an apology. I have written what follows from the

---

5 "Of the Sufficiency of the Holy Scriptures for Salvation."

point of view of the "straight centre" of the Anglican Communion, for it appears that this is where decisions of importance are made. I wish to address that decision-making centre of the church because I believe the people it represents should be encouraged to do a lot of rethinking. This stylistic orientation may create the impression that I am talking *about* the Anglican homosexual community rather than *to* them or *with* them, as though its members were not really present but were in the narthex while the discussion was going on in the chancel, as though they were not fully accepted even in this conversation, which is partly about them. This is not my intention. All of us in the Anglican Communion have an obligation to take up these issues afresh, as equal members of this tradition-treasuring but wonderfully flexible Communion, giving thanks that while the gospel does not change in its message of liberation and transformation, the details vary in accordance with the challenges of each context.

A biographical note: I was born and spent my childhood in conservative sectarian Christianity in which biblical literalism and infallibility were taken for granted. After a short period of non-observance, I became an Anglican at the age of sixteen, more than fifty years ago at the time of writing, and began a long and sometimes painful journey towards an understanding of the Bible that is, I believe, not only authentically Anglican but deeper and more honest than unquestioning literalism can ever be. I am grateful to the Evangelical wing of Anglicanism because it made my transition from extreme fundamentalism possible. I am grateful to the Anglo-Catholic movement for the rich mixture of symbolism and social responsibility to which it introduced me. I am grateful to modernist Anglicanism for its hospitality to the questioning and sceptical mind and its daring pursuit of truth that is relevant to the current context. Most of all, I am grateful for the intensely reverent but temperate and cautious approach to the Bible, which is reflected in some of our basic doctrinal and liturgical documents. I do not want to see this great insight and tradition eclipsed or modified.

I have not included in the following pages an analysis of the passages in the Bible that are understood to refer to homosexuality. Commentaries abound, reflecting various points of view, and readers may consult them.[6] My concern is theological: the nature of biblical authority, as well as the ways in which we use the Bible and the cultural dynamics that help to shape that process. I am concerned that the Lambeth Conference resolution on the Bible may encourage in some quarters a simplistic use of biblical texts in a pattern known colloquially as "proof-texting," that is, the rhetorical use of texts out of context, without reference to the "main drift"[7] of the biblical pattern, and with weight that is drawn from the importance attached to the argument in which they are used rather than their place in the whole biblical record. And, because of the proximity of this resolution to the statement on sexuality, I am concerned that a sensitive issue will be treated as settled before a real examination of the matter has properly begun. Our reverence for the Bible demands much more of us than this.

---

6 See the treatment of Genesis 18.26—19.29, Leviticus 18.22, 20.13, Deuteronomy 23.17–18, Romans 1.18–32, 1 Corinthians 6.9–10, 1 Timothy 1.8–11, and Jude 7 in Michael Vasey, *Strangers and Friends: A new exploration of homosexuality and the Bible*, Hodder and Stoughton, London, 1995, pp. 124–138, and related footnotes. For another perspective, see Marion L. Soards, *Scipture and Homosexuality: Biblical authority and the church today*, Westminster John Knox Press, Louisville, Kentucky, 1995.

7 The term is Richard Hooker's. See chapter 5.

I have already referred to the Thirty-nine Articles and will later discuss what they have to say about the Bible. A few words of explanation of the history of the role of the Articles may be helpful for some readers.

The Articles are a series of doctrinal statements that were produced in the sixteenth century at a time of significant theological controversy in the newly independent Church of England. Most of the churches of the Reformation period expressed their theological positions in statements known as "confessions," like the Protestant confessions of Augsburg (1530) and Westminster (1643), and even the Roman Catholic Catechism of Pius V (1568) which reflected the decisions of the Council of Trent. These statements are fuller than creeds, but less detailed than the great collections of argument in which medieval theologians outlined their positions, and there is good reason to believe that the Thirty-nine Articles were intended by some to be an Anglican confession. However, because of the controversial nature of the Anglican reformation and the intention of national and church leaders to maintain one church for one country, the Articles became in some measure an instrument of compromise that allowed differing parties to survive in the same house rather than to exclude one another entirely.

English law at first required clergy and members of the universities of Oxford and Cambridge to "subscribe" to the Articles, but the Church of England *in practice* never really accepted the Articles with the heartfelt enthusiasm that stricter Protestants accorded their confessions. By the 1650s, Archbishop Bramhall could write that no one was required to believe the Articles, only not to teach otherwise. Anglicans *in practice* turned to the *Book of Common Prayer* as a major basis of doctrine, and the Prayer Book, reinforced somewhat by the Articles, functioned as a theological compass to Anglicans as they made their way on hitherto uncharted waters.[8] If you wanted to know the position of the church on some subject, you started by looking up references to that subject in the Prayer Book.[9]

There is an Anglican principle that the faith of the church is based on Scripture, tradition, and reason. It is an essentially dynamic principle because it assumes interaction among these bases of belief, and between them and the present context. Scripture and tradition are not imposed in isolation from each other: Scripture is, in fact, the most basic stratum of tradition, and tradition, as it developed in the writings, councils, and worship of the church, as the unfolding of its understanding of the scriptures. Nor are Scripture and tradition invoked unimaginatively, but sensibly (with reason), and with a view to their meaning here and now.

The Thirty-nine Articles must be seen against this background and in this framework. They are not the last word on

---

8 Bramhall's words are, "We do not suffer any man 'to reject' the Thirty-nine articles of the Church of England 'at his pleasure'; yet neither do we look upon them as essentials of serving faith or 'legacies of Christ and His Apostles'; but in a mean, as pious opinions fitted for the presentation of unity. Neither do we oblige any man to believe them, but only not to contradict them." From *Schism Guarded*, I.xi, in Paul Elmer More and Frank Leslie Cross, *Anglicanism*, London, SPCK, 1962, p. 186.

9 To this day I would respond to a request for the Anglican "position" on any theological subject by examining first its treatment in the various Prayer Books—1549 as well as 1662, and other provincial variants like the Canadian books of 1922 and 1962. Second, I would see what the XXXIX Articles said on the subject. Only after determining these roots of our tradition would I explore treatment of the subject in subsequent Anglican history, in writings of theological opinion, theological commission reports, modern liturgical texts, Lambeth Conference and Anglican Consultative Council reports, as well as synodical decisions and current contextual explorations.

any subject, but they are an important word because they provide a "snapshot" of critical doctrinal positions at a formative period in Anglican development and in relation to the disputes of that particular time. When they are consulted in conjunction with the formularies of the Prayer Book (tradition distilled in the form of worship), they provide a partial but helpful picture of the path that has brought Anglicans to the present. Of course, the story is not over. Traditional Anglican forms of worship are changing as I write, but one hopes and trusts that on significant matters their change will be consistent with the major milestones on the way, even as they lead across cultural horizons we cannot imagine and find new and unexpected forms of expression. But this is another story for another time.

I am grateful to friends who read and commented on my manuscript, in particular Margaret and Ted Offerman, Robert Maclennan, Greig Dunn, John Martin, Jim Rosenthal, Michael Thompson, William Crockett, Sister Thelma Anne, SSJD, Oriole Burton, and others. Some of them provided detailed suggestions that have been very helpful in the process of revision. The faults, however, remain mine.

1
Culture, Perception, and the Lambeth Conference

NEARLY THIRTY-FIVE years ago, Harvey Cox, an American Baptist scholar, dropped a bombshell into the world of theology. His seminal book, *The Secular City*, challenged traditional Christians to come to terms with the cultural change that was already overwhelming the urbanized world, and to explore the eclipse of traditional religion and the future of their faith. Cox wrote at a time of great theological ferment. *The Secular City* was published only two years after John Robinson's *Honest to God*, and appeared in the same climate of thought as the "God is dead" movement. It looked dangerous. But for many Christians who were struggling with the reality that a traditional theological arm wouldn't go into a new cultural sleeve, his book had a quality both positive and refreshing. He didn't ask us to throw our faith away; he asked us to come to terms with our context and discover what our faith had to say in this new forum.

To provide a time frame for the exploration of the emerging culture, Cox painted a triptych of human history. Human culture was first of all based on the *tribe*, then on the *town*, and then on the *secular city*.

Tribal culture is grounded on kinship. It is a secure world of known values and traditions, closed to all that is foreign and different. It answers most of the great questions of life before they are asked. It finds expression in myth, story, and dance—and also, I would add, in ritual and taboo. The tribe lives in the individual as much as the individual lives in the tribe.

Town life appears when tribes have to live together whether they want to or not, when war or famine or some other external force makes the continued insulation of the tribe impossible. Then the private gods of the tribe are replaced by overarching civic deities, barter is replaced by coinage, the custom of the elders is replaced by the lawbook of the magistrate, the memory of the storyteller is replaced by writing, the insight of myth is replaced by systems of belief supported by rational argument. The long *hidden* history of humanity is tribal. The shorter *known* history of humanity is the story of towns and cities, from Nineveh and Jerusalem and Athens and Rome of ancient history, to London and Paris of the age of the Enlightenment. It is ultimately the story of *humanism*, that wonderful development of a human community in which knowledge could be expanded and nature subjugated. But it is a community very different in quality from the cohesive tribe: ultimately, the culture of the town confers independence and individuality, those hallmarks of classical liberalism.

Cox may have referred to tribe, town, and secular city as stages in human development, and no doubt they were. But they also describe styles of culture and ways in which knowledge and perception are grasped and shared. Tribal culture is not by definition backward, nor is it limited to certain races; it may (and often does) include layers of exquisite sophistication.

Town culture is not necessarily stodgy or self-satisfied; it has provided the environment for some of the greatest human achievements. Secular culture is certainly not necessarily better or ideal: its astringent atmosphere is too thin for some who find themselves within its fold. We are talking about three different ways in which the communities of humanity perceive reality and engage with it, ways that have had a sequential history but now exist side by side.

For Cox, the secular city is a third phase in this process. The secular city is not just the town grown bigger: indeed, I suggest that the secular city is not a place at all but a culture through which people understand their world, whether they live in a physical metropolis or in relative isolation. The word *secular* is derived from the Latin for *age* or *times*; since the middle of the nineteenth century it has been used to affirm that the world, as we find it in the age in which we live, provides the context in which we will discover whatever explanations there may be. As an adjective, *secular* describes a culture in which there is no consensus that this world is controlled by another world (the stars, the gods), or that one system of thinking (Aristotle, Confucius) has an unquestionable claim on the human mind.

Surprisingly, secularity, in this sense of the word, is very much a product of the Jewish-Christian tradition, which has contributed to the de-sacralizing of the natural order and in consequence to the seriousness with which it is taken in itself. Our scriptures record a steady movement away from the notion that nature is inherently sacred. The Elijah story provides an example. When Elijah stood before the entrance to the cave on the holy mountain, he witnessed a violent windstorm, an earthquake, and a fire, the signs of nature deities, but God was not in those phenomena. It was the "sound of sheer silence" that made him wrap his face in his cloak and stand at the door of his cave.[10] The natural order is neither haunted nor enchanted. It is simply there.

There is a parallel movement away from the notion that divine law is in the heavens towards belief that its proper place is in the human heart. Moses tells the people of Israel that the law he has given them,

> is not in heaven, that you should say, "Who will go up to heaven for us, and get it for us that we may hear it and observe it?' Neither is it beyond the sea, that you should say, "Who will cross to the other side of the sea for us, and get it for us so that we may hear it and observe it?" No, the word is very near to you; it is in your mouth and in your heart for you to observe.[11]

The prophet Jeremiah similarly looked forward to a new covenant when God would (the voice is God's),

> put my law within them, and I will write it on their hearts; and I will be their God, and they shall be my people. No longer shall they teach one another, or say to each other, "Know the Lord," for they shall all know me.[12]

There is a third movement away from the notion that a distant God may be placated by ritual and taboo towards belief that the sacred is to be encountered in actions of compassion and justice. The prophet Amos attacked the temple cult with its

---

10   1 Kings 19.11ff.
11   Deuteronomy 30.12–14
12   Jeremiah 31.33f

rich, musical liturgy and offerings of grain and animals. "Take away from me the noise of your songs," he wrote (the voice is God's), "I will not listen to the melody of your harps. But let justice roll down like waters, and righteousness like an everflowing stream."[13] The prophet Micah similarly asked what he had to do to "get right" with God—offer thousands of rams, rivers of oil, even sacrifice his firstborn son? He replied, "What does the Lord require of you but to do justice, and to love kindness, and to walk humbly with your God."[14] The author of the closing section of the book we know by the name of Isaiah addressed people who could not understand why God did not respond to their ritual fasting in a time of trouble. He replied (again the voice is God's),

> Is not this the fast that I choose: to loose the bonds of
> injustice, to undo the thongs of the yoke, to let the
> oppressed go free, and to break every yoke? Is it not
> to share your bread with the hungry and bring the
> homeless poor into your house; when you see the
> naked, to cover them, and not to hide yourself from
> your own kin? Then your light shall break forth like
> the dawn, and your healing shall spring up quickly.[15]

These are shifts in emphasis and understanding, shifts away from notions of the sacred as the property of another time and place that are greater than the ordinary world in which we live, and towards an appreciation of the paramount importance of the present time and place, the present *saeculum*, or age. Such shifts

---

13 Amos 5.23–24
14 Micah 6.8
15 Isaiah 58.6–8b

do not in themselves define exhaustively the word *secular* as we understand it, but together with a Jewish interpretation of history as the sphere of divine-human encounter, they laid the groundwork for future secular culture.

Cox described secular life with four words: he said it is anonymous, mobile, pragmatic, and profane, in contrast with tribal and town life, which had tended to involve living in stable and settled communities that were tied together by systems of belief or commonly held ideals.

Secular life is *anonymous*: Cox uses the image of someone at a giant switchboard making decisions and connections for people he or she never sees. If he had waited a few decades, he could have pictured this anonymity in terms of the solitary midnight browser surfing across the continents of the internet, in touch with the notes, articles, messages, even thoughts of thousands of people he or she will never meet. The global village that the cybernetic revolution has created is really a metropolis of hundreds of millions of people who are all invisible to one another in sterilized relationships outside of the pattern of ordinary sense experience. Nameless solitude in a vast crowd is a characteristic of secular life.

Secular life is *mobile*: Cox pictures the driver on a motorway interchange where everyone is in rapid motion to and from destinations unknown to one another. He refers to the ease with which people follow jobs from place to place in contrast to tribal humanity and its attachment to its sacred places. Tribal culture is often defined by geography. "The people," as tribes often call themselves, live between these two rivers or encircled by those four mountains and everywhere else is less real. Town culture also assumes stability—even when it is disrupted. Thornton Wilder's *Our Town* captures a sense that being born, growing up, marrying, and dying on the same street or even in the same house is a virtue. In the secular city people expect to move. It is a sign of success that your company sends you to Hong Kong or a university far away recruits you to its staff.

Secular life is *pragmatic*: it is concerned with practical and workable solutions rather than with the imposition of a grand ideology. Apartheid was imposed in South Africa as an ideological solution based on elaborate racial theories and undergirded by a carefully crafted (if perverse) theology. I visited South Africa after apartheid had been abandoned but before Nelson Mandela was elected, and I heard a minister in the last National government say that apartheid was abandoned because "it did not work." He did not say it was abandoned because it was wrong but because it was not pragmatically sound.

And secular life is *profane*: it is lived "outside the temple" (which is what *profane* means), without any universally recognized sacred order to define it. The secular city does not necessarily condemn religion. Indeed many contemporary people in the secular culture are devout believers, and many search in the byways of religion for a pattern of symbolism, reflection, inner depth, and commitment that will meet a genuine religious hunger. But secular life does not need or recognize a single religious system to give it cohesion.

Many people in the 1960s thought that Cox and other creative theologians of the time were proposing that Christianity disappear by imploding itself into negation. This was not the case. They were asking Christians to look at the emerging culture surrounding them and ask what the gospel has to say in this context. For if we really do believe that Christianity has an abiding message, then it will have an abiding message that makes sense even in the secular culture in which we live. Recognition of the reality of the secular culture (the culture of this *saeculum*, or age, which is *our* age) does not mean that one must abandon Christianity. It means, however, that one recognizes oneself as a secular Christian and not a tribal or medieval Christian.

Much of what Cox described in *The Secular City* as a possible future is now accepted fact, although Cox much later revealed that he was surprised by the durability of religious phenomena.[16] Many of the details of our contemporary life illustrate his thesis, although not necessarily as he expected. What Cox called *secularity* is now often referred to as *post-modernism*, a term that defines a culture that sees itself as cut off historically from the assumptions of town life in general and from the world-view of the Enlightenment in particular.[17]

So-called "modern" or Enlightenment thought, the crown and conclusion of the whole thrust of centuries of town life culture, found expression in the notion of progress and the goal of human perfection, which were to be achieved through science and reason. At a popular level at least, there was a sense that everything might eventually be known and understood and consequently controlled, that science would provide an overarching system, not only of explanation but also of solution, bringing not only industrial efficiency and medical

---

16 "The Myth of the Twentieth Century: The rise and fall of secularisation," in *Harvard Divinity Bulletin*, 1998, vol. 28.

17 Twenty-five years after the publication of *The Secular City*, Cox wrote, "Was *The Secular City* a harbinger of post-modernism, as one writer recently suggested? The word itself did not exist then, and I am not sure I know what it means today. But if it suggests a willingness to live with a certain pragmaticism and provisionality, a suspicion of all-encompassing schemes, a readiness to risk a little more disorder instead of a little too much *Ordnung*, then I think the book qualifies." "*The Secular City* 25 Years Later," in *The Christian Century*, Nov. 7, 1990, p. 1029.

intervention (two very real and valuable contributions of the scientific age) but peace and goodwill and universal harmony.

The heady optimism of modern thought was severely challenged by the two major wars that dominated the first half of the twentieth century, by the holocaust, by the Viet Nam war and its insidious effect on many of those who were recruited to participate in it, and by poverty, famine, hunger, and the exploitation of both people and environment, which all appear to be impervious to reform in spite of incredible technological achievement and profound theoretical analysis. The miracles of polio vaccination and organ transplants are shadowed by the nightmares of nuclear weapons and nerve gas.

Post-modern thought is simply more cautious. It resists the premise that any "body of knowledge, or subject of knowledge, constitutes a unified totality."[18] Unlike classical science, post-modern thought cannot accept claims that any intellectual discourse is disinterested or pure and has no hidden or even unconscious agendas. Post-modern thought is suspicious of stories or narratives (sometimes called "metanarratives") that provide a general theory or explanation of the nature and destiny of humanity. Post-modernists wilfully transgress the accepted boundaries of supposed departments of knowledge, believing that knowledge cannot be imprisoned in watertight compartments, each under the authority of specialists qualified in that field. Post-modernists resist the notion that a word or image or icon can "freeze" a particular understanding of reality forever, believing on the contrary that everything changes

---

18 See my paper, "Postmodern biblical criticism: A key to post-modern liturgical criticism," in *Open, Journal of the Associated Parishes for Liturgy and Mission*, Spring and Summer, 1997. I am indebted to A.K.M. Adam, *What is Postmodern Biblical Criticism?*, Fortress Press, 1995, for this sketch of post-modern thought.

in the course of time. Post-modern criticism treats historical reconstructions with some suspicion, recognizing that they have all been based on data that were partial, were selected by people whose point of view was necessarily biased one way or another, and may reflect the assumptions of social structure and relationship (that is, power) of the communities for which they were produced. Post-modern thought resists the notion that any system of knowledge is absolute.

At first glance this reticence on the part of post-modern thought appears to set it on a path of conflict with Christian faith. And from the point of view of many orthodox Christians of the town life era of human history, and especially those of the Enlightenment period, this is so. Christians in the age of science looked at the body of positive knowledge that science had generated and made the claim that their fundamental tenets were just as true and demanding. It is not surprising that the term "fundamentalism" as we know it was created by a group of conservative Protestant leaders in the early years of the twentieth century, in reaction to tendencies among other Christians that were perceived to be modernist. (The fundamental points of doctrine on which no ground could be given were the virgin birth, the physical resurrection of Jesus, the infallibility of the scriptures, the substitutionary nature of the atonement, and the physical second coming of Jesus.) There is a sense in which fundamentalism as the assertion of literal and absolute truth could only exist in an environment in which science had set the standard of such truth. Fundamentalism is the delinquent child of modernism.

On the other hand, there is every reason why Christians should welcome the humility of the post-modernist climate. One of the most important texts in the Bible is the *Sh'ma*, recited daily by Jews and a frequent part of the Anglican eucharist for more than two hundred years. "Hear, O Israel! The Lord our God, the Lord is one," it begins. These words do not mean that God is one as opposed to twelve or sixteen. They have no bearing on the Christian doctrine of the Trinity. They mean that God is one as distinct from the multiplicity of everything else. In the words of a more frequent translation, "The Lord is our God, the Lord alone." In short, there is no absolute but the Absolute—nothing, not tradition, not the creeds, not the Bible, not the church, not the *Book of Common Prayer*, not the Lambeth Conference, can be treated as though it modified that absolute unity—and any introduction of other absolutes is superstition and idolatry. There are many things in this world that point to the Centre of Being, things that hint at the nature of God, but they are not the Centre. That combination of compassion and responsibility that we call love is as close as we can get to saying, "This is God," but we Christians do so only because we believe God has been so exposed (revealed) in Jesus as the Christ, and not because love is something other than God, which we may treat as absolute. The post-modernists are right: beware of absolutes.

Whatever the word *God* may mean, in good biblical theology it does not mean an overarching explanation of reality. That is the God of the eighteenth-century Deists, the clockmaker who has gone home for the night, the designer of the garden who has retired to a distant apartment upstairs. The God of the Bible is much more elusive than that, and the God of Christian theism is much more paradoxical than that.[19] By Theism I mean

19 See Samuel Therrien, *The Elusive Presence: Toward a New Biblical Theology*, Harper and Row, San Francisco, 1978, especially, "It is when presence escapes man's grasp that it surges, survives, or returns. It is also when human beings meet in social responsibility that presence, once vanished, is heard," p. 476.

the belief not only that God is beyond, but also that God is equally and simultaneously within, the sacred Centre that transcends and infuses. God is beyond, not as the final answer or solution to the cosmic puzzle but as the infinite mystery,[20] relativizing all our partial answers and descriptions. God is within, not as the soul of a pantheistic universe, but, in Meister Eckhart's terms, as the Circle whose centre is everywhere and circumference nowhere. Or in the words of Mordecai Kaplan, the founder of Reconstructionist Judaism, God is the power of salvation running through the universe—now here, now there, inexplicably, unexpectedly, in personal relationships, in social change, in liberation of the oppressed in body, mind, or estate, and often at great distance from the religious institutions that claim to speak for God. There is no conflict between postmodernist reticence and humility, and a cautious and reverent use of the word *God*.

In many ways those who are trying to hear what the Gospel is saying to a secular age have more in common with tribal culture than with the modernist town life culture from which they have more immediately sprung. The tribe and the secular city are both prepared to express their thoughts and feelings in malleable, flexible, dynamic, pre-rational forms—in images, icons, poetry, ritual, even play—while town life culture is more tied to its lawgiver and philosopher foundations. But they have less in common when it comes to treating received tradition as absolute. A tribal point of view tends to emphasize, "as it was in the beginning, is now, and ever shall be," as the stuff that holds a people together, come what may. A secular point of view recognizes that each day may bring challenges we have not met

---

20 Which is the meaning of Elijah's awe before the sound of sheer silence.

before and for which we do not have ready-made answers, but this is no cause for fear. The tradition will give us light, but we still have to find the answer.

An American bishop, well known for his liberal point of view, suggested in an interview in the summer of 1998 that members of a certain group holding a certain position that they intended to pursue at the then future Lambeth Conference were superstitious. It was a mistake. Since the group to which he referred was identifiable by geography, race, and colour, he provoked a strong reaction and eventually he had to apologize. One may sympathize with his critics: a tribal viewpoint should not be dismissed as necessarily primitive and undeveloped or inherently deficient. It is one way in which a vast body of knowledge, experience, and wisdom may be conserved for the benefit of a people. On the other hand, the Latin *superstitio* carries the meaning of an undue, excessive, irrational fear of the sacred, and may be distinguished from *religio*, which is an appropriate, balanced, and sensible attitude to the sacred. It is difficult for those who believe that every human practice must be open to review in the light of the Gospel to communicate creatively with those who hold that certain traditions are absolute and beyond discussion and that touching them is forbidden.

In the summer of 1998 the chickens of Cox's prophetic analysis came home to roost for the Anglican Communion. Everyone came to the Lambeth Conference with the knowledge that homosexuality and the ecclesial status of persons living in committed and loving homosexual relationships would preoccupy the attention of the Conference.[21] Cox's scheme may not

---

21 No one, no matter how liberal, suggested that the Conference or anyone else should approve of promiscuous homosexuality, any more than they would have approved of promiscuous heterosexuality.

be the last word on cultural history, but the subject of homosexuality did in fact sort the bishops more or less in accordance with his threefold description.

One group clearly represented cultures and societies with a fixed and traditional point of view, in which the reality of homosexuality had been contained and controlled for centuries if not millennia. They were literally unable to discuss the subject, except to refuse to discuss it. Some of them threatened to leave the Conference if they were asked to meet and listen to real, live homosexual Christians. One suggested that the contact would be "polluting." Another attempted to exorcise forcibly and in public a person he understood to be homosexual. They treated homosexuality as a taboo area of human experience and behaviour, and some of them compared it to other practices that have attracted general disapproval, like sexual congress with animals. Some of them expressed genuine concern about the effect a more liberal stance on this subject would have on their Muslim neighbours. Some of them denied that homosexuality is a universal phenomenon, appearing in a more or less constant percentage of the human race, irrespective of race. They described it as a "white man's disease," which had been imported to other societies. Of course, the biblical texts on homosexuality appeared to reinforce the positions held in this group. There seemed to be little recognition of the various ways in which homosexuality has been checked and suppressed in various cultures that find it threatening.

On this last point, it is my opinion that homosexuality is very threatening to societies that have a history or tradition of arranged marriage and child or adolescent marriage, and especially in combination. Arranged marriages are frequently the external sign of property alignments, and their stability is important for the maintenance of family and social structures.

Where late-developing awareness of sexual identity results in dissatisfaction with the marriage and, even worse, in limiting the production of children, it is bound to be seen as socially and not merely sexually perverse. A rigid reaction to homosexuality in such societies is consequently understandable even if not commendable.

A second group, probably representing a centrist position of Anglican thought, based its disapproval of homosexuality primarily on a number of biblical texts. This group was, in fact, using the Bible as a source of law, in the spirit of town life culture, which has always looked to the law and the lawgiver for, the rational regulation of its social life. Whether the Bible, even on its own terms, can bear the freight that this position loads on it remains to be seen, but there are many who believe it can, and their point of view tends to reinforce the prejudice (I use this word in its technical sense to mean *judging before the trial begins*) of those who treat the subject as forbidden. In any case, in order to express disapproval of homosexuality and base this rejection on what appeared to be solid ground, two resolutions with a somewhat circular relationship were necessary. The first reinforces the Bible as a source of law, and the second appeals to the Bible to make its case on sexuality. Without the first, the second would have lost force, and without the second (given traditional Anglican commitment to the Bible), the first might have lacked point. These resolutions are so central to the work of the 1998 Lambeth Conference (and to the coalition of tribal and town life points of view) that they must be quoted in full.

The resolution on the Authority of Holy Scriptures (III.5) reads,

This Conference
(a) affirms that our creator God, transcendent as well as immanent, communicates with us authoritatively through the Holy Scriptures of the Old and New Testaments; and
(b) in agreement with the Lambeth Quadrilateral,[22] and in solidarity with the Lambeth Conference of 1888, affirms that these Holy Scriptures contain 'all things necessary to salvation' and are for us the 'rule and ultimate standard' of faith and practice.

The resolution on Human Sexuality (I.10) reads,

This Conference
(a) commends to the Church the subsection report on human sexuality;
(b) in view of the teaching of Scripture, upholds faithfulness in marriage between a man and a woman in life-

---

22 The so-called Lambeth Quadrilateral, a proposal of four essential pillars for a reunited Christianity, originated at the General Convention of the Episcopal Church (USA) in 1886. It was modified slightly by the Lambeth Conference of 1888. The full text reads, "A. The Holy Scriptures of the Old and New Testaments, as 'containing all things necessary to salvation', and as being the rule and ultimate standard of faith. B. The Apostles' Creed, as the Baptismal Symbol; and the Nicene Creed, as the sufficient statement of the Christian Faith. C. The two Sacraments ordained by Christ himself—Baptism and the Supper of the Lord—ministered with unfailing use of Christ's Words of Institution, and of the elements ordained by Him. D. The Historic Episcopate, locally adapted in the methods of its administration to the varying needs of the nations and peoples called of God into the Unity of his Church." Note that the words "and practice" in III.5.b of Lambeth 1998 do not appear in section A in the 1888 form of the Lambeth Quadrilateral.

long union, and believes that abstinence is right for those who are not called to marriage;

(c) recognises that there are among us persons who experience themselves as having a homosexual orientation. Many of these are members of the Church and are seeking the pastoral care, moral direction of the Church, and God's transforming power for the living of their lives and the ordering of relationships. We commit ourselves to listen to the experience of homosexual persons and we wish to assure them that they are loved by God and that all baptised, believing and faithful persons, regardless of sexual orientation, are full members of the Body of Christ;

(d) while rejecting homosexual practice as incompatible with Scripture, calls on all our people to minister pastorally and sensitively to all irrespective of sexual orientation and to condemn irrational fear of homosexuals, violence within marriage and any trivialisation and commercialisation of sex;

(e) cannot advise the legitimising or blessing of same sex unions nor ordaining those involved in same gender unions;

(f) requests the Primates and the ACC to establish a means of monitoring the work done on the subject of human sexuality in the Communion and to share statements and resources among us;

(g) notes the significance of the Kuala Lumpur Statement on Human Sexuality and the concerns expressed in resolutions IV.26, V.1, V10, V.23, and V.35 on the authority of Scripture in matters of marriage and sexuality and asks the Primates and the ACC to include them in their monitoring process.

In the context of the 1998 Lambeth Conference, the key points in the resolution on sexuality are that homosexuals may be good Christians but their sexual practice, if any, is incompatible with Scripture and their committed relationships should therefore not be legitimized and those so related should not be ordained. These points are proposed within the framework of a complicated resolution that affirms faithfulness in marriage and abstinence for the unmarried, commits members of the Conference to listening to the experience of homosexuals and to fostering pastoral care irrespective of sexual orientation, and condemns sexual violence, trivialization, and commercialization, as well as "irrational fear of homosexuals." (This latter point is particularly surprising in view of the fact that historically homosexuals have had much more to fear from the majority "straight" community, which has done little to protect them from vilification, physical abuse, mockery, and prejudice affecting employment.) The request in (g) that the Primates and the ACC include the Kuala Lumpur Statement on Human Sexuality and a number of resolutions proposed at the Conference in their process of monitoring work in the Communion on the subject of sexuality is remarkable and peculiar because it gives an extraordinary dignity and status to resolutions that were otherwise bypassed, defeated, or withdrawn in the legislative process of the Conference itself. This peculiarity adheres *especially* to the Kuala Lumpur document (a traditional and conservative statement produced by an informal gathering of Anglican leaders from a number of provinces in non-Western cultural settings) in view of the fact that the Conference twice considered resolutions which would have approved it in one way or another and agreed to pass to the next item of business.[23]

---

23 See appendix for the *Kuala Lumpur Statement on Human Sexuality.*

The words "incompatible with Scripture" are central to this resolution and its thrust, and they look necessarily to the resolution on the Authority of Holy Scripture and its claim that God "communicates with us authoritatively through the Holy Scriptures of the Old and New Testaments." This claim raises many more questions than it solves. Does God communicate with us through all Holy Scripture uniformly or in some parts of it more than others? Who decides? What is meant by "communicates"? Does this give the Bible the status of a system of law? And, if so, who is to interpret? How does this word "communicates" relate to the concept of the Bible as the "Word of God"—a less brittle and much more iconic and subtle concept, as I hope to show. And, in any case, are we quite sure we know exactly what we mean by "Holy Scriptures"?

The resolution on the Authority of Holy Scriptures is also open to some suspicion of obfuscation. The first clause affirms that God communicates with us authoritatively through the Holy Scriptures. The second clause professes agreement with the Lambeth Quadrilateral on a very different and much more traditionally Anglican understanding of the place of Scripture. These two clauses should not be read as though they were connected, or as though one were the development of the other. There is no reason to conclude that the authors of the Lambeth Quadrilateral and of Resolution 11 of Lambeth 1888 would necessarily have been comfortable with the first clause of the 1998 resolution.

Traditional Anglican theology on Scripture, articulated in the ordinals and in Article VI of the Thirty-nine Articles, is content to say that Scripture contains all things necessary for salvation and that nothing may be taught as necessary for salvation that cannot be proved from Scripture. It is a very different thing to claim that Scripture is the medium of divine communication, suggesting that inspiration is verbal, consisting of discrete messages, perhaps even a matter of "automatic writing" through the historical biblical authors, and implying that *any* biblical prescription might be enforced as absolute. It is difficult not to wonder if an attempt has been made to bring a very guarded Anglican tradition on Holy Scripture, worded in general terms ("contains all things necessary"), or negatively in terms of what may *not* be done with the Bible, within the compass of a much more rigid and literalist interpretation of its role.

Clearly some reflection on our literary tradition is necessary before we can consider its application to the specific problem of homosexuality. What are the Holy Scriptures? What is the Bible? What do we mean when we call it the "Word of God"? What is its authority? Do tribal, town life, and postmodern (secular) cultures have different ways of understanding what the Bible is? How does the Bible "communicate"? These questions will shape the direction of the chapters that follow.

2

How We Use the Bible

EVERYONE KNOWS WHAT the Bible is. It is that book, often bound in black leather, that is read in church and studied by the devout. Most people know that it contains a number of smaller books, which are in turn divided into chapters and verses. They also know that it is divided into two main sections, called the Old and New Testaments.

Jews, of course, do not recognize the New Testament, so there are really two bibles.

The Old Testament in a Roman Catholic Bible contains thirty-nine smaller books, which are called "protocanonical" because they were accepted with little or no debate. In addition, Roman Catholics recognize several "deuterocanonical" books (often known as the *Apocrypha*) as equal to the others. Most Protestants have rejected these books. The (Presbyterian) Westminster Confession (1648) dismissed them as, "not being of divine inspiration ... and therefore of no authority to the Church of God."[24]

---

24 For a general introduction to the subject of the canon or standard of what constitutes the Bible and how it grew, see Raymond E. Brown and Raymond F. Collins, "Canonicity," in *The New Jerome Biblical Commentary*, Geoffrey Chapman, London, pp. 1034–1054.

Now there are three bibles.

Anglicans recognize both the protocanonical and deutero-canonical books, but in different ways. Article VI of the Thirty-nine Articles distinguishes between those books, "of whose authority was never any doubt in the Church," and "the other Books ... the Church doth read for example of life and instruction of manners; but yet doth it not apply them to establish any doctrine." In practice, the deuterocanonical or Apocryphal books fell into some disfavour among Anglicans and in 1827 the British and Foreign Bible Society stopped printing them. Some Anglicans are still wary of them. However, they have continued to appear in Anglican lectionaries, at least as optional readings, and they provide some of the canticles of Anglican liturgy (like the *Benedicite Omnia Opera* and *The Souls of the Righteous*). The Bible presented to me at my ordination in St. Paul's Cathedral, London, in 1957 contains the Apocrypha.

Now there are something like three-and-a-half bibles.

The Orthodox (Byzantine) church is somewhat divided on this subject. The Greek church recognizes the longer list, while some Russian theologians do not accept the Apocrypha. Both Copts and Ethiopians (Oriental Orthodox) have included not only the deuterocanonical writings but also additional apocryphal material not included by others, although what status they give it is not clear.

There is now an unknown number of bibles.

Behind this confusion is the fact that the Jewish scriptures (what Christians call the Old Testament) exist in two major versions, one in Hebrew and the other in Greek. Obviously the Hebrew version is older, but the Greek version (a translation known as the *Septuagint*, which was undertaken at Alexandria for the large expatriate Jewish community there) had great stature. It was material in the *Septuagint* that did not appear in the

Hebrew text that formed the basis of the deuterocanonical writings. Although Western Christians know the "protocanonical" Jewish scriptures in translation from the Hebrew, the authors of the New Testament mostly quoted from the Greek *Septuagint* and it is still in liturgical use in the Greek-speaking churches.

How many bibles are there now?

It is important to note that in addition to these divergences in the form of the Bible as we know it, there is also a wealth of varying manuscript evidence that has been sifted and sorted to produce the text on which our translations are based. The Introduction in my Greek New Testament includes more than twenty pages of lists of manuscripts in which the Christian scriptures have been transmitted, all of them carefully sorted by type and period. Every page in that edition of the Greek New Testament is divided between text and a list of manuscripts in which various readings of the text appear, and the degree of certainty of the reading adopted is graded on a scale of one-to-four. The lists of variants often occupy one-third of their page, and sometimes more than half.[25]

It is clear that the authority of the Bible cannot be based on the existence of a single, discrete, immutable, unvarying text. Christians have obviously never been in complete agreement on what they meant by "Holy Scriptures." The various Christian divisions, which began in earnest in the fourth and fifth centuries and became more serious with the division, first, of East and West and then with the shattering of Western

25   Kurt Aland, Matthew Black, Bruce M. Metzger, Allen Wikgren, eds., *The Greek New Testament*, American Bible Society, British and Foreign Bible Society, National Bible Society of Scotland, Netherlands Bible Society, Württemberg Bible Society, 1966.

Christianity in the period of the Reformation, allowed various churches to claim their bible as the true bible and to treat variants with suspicion or contempt. This is less possible in our ecumenical age.

The authority of the Bible is also challenged by the internal contradictions it contains. It is true that Article XX[26] of the Anglican Thirty-nine Articles rules that the church may not, "so expound one place of Scripture, that it be repugnant to another," but this defence suggests not only locking the barn door after the horse has been stolen but also claiming that the door had never been unlocked in the first place. It does not take too much imagination to recognize that there is some tension between Mark's picture of a very human Jesus who says to a supplicant, "Why do you call me good? No one is good but God alone,"[27] and John's interpretation of Jesus as the eternal, pre-existent Word made flesh, who states plainly, "The Father and I are one." Nor is it hard to find differences between Paul's statement, "We hold that a person is justified by faith apart from works prescribed by the law,"[28] and James's, "Faith by itself, if it has no works, is dead."[29]

A more critical example is provided by the fifth commandment, "Honour your father and your mother, so that your days may be long in the land that the Lord your God is giving you." Jewish commentators emphasize the importance of this commandment, which alone among the ten has a promise attached to it. As the fifth commandment it appears on the first tablet—

---

26 "Of the Authority of the Church."
27 Mark 10.18.
28 Romans 3.28.
29 James 2.17.

the tablet of obligations to God.[30] And yet, according to the gospels, Jesus challenged this commandment (more, perhaps, than any other) with the words, "Whoever comes to me and does not hate father and mother, wife and children, brothers and sisters, yes, and even life itself, cannot be my disciple."[31] In a situation in which a traditional patriarchal family system could be stifling, Jesus opted for the relative independence of his movement and described his followers as "my mother and my brothers,"[32] and said that "My mother and my brothers are those who hear the word of God and do it."[33]

Another kind of contradiction appears in the possibility that the Bible actually contains controversy and that some parts of the Bible may have been written to confront or correct other parts. For instance, the books of Ezra and Nehemiah reflect a period of national reconstruction during which a conservative religious leadership not only denounced marriages that Jews had contracted with people of other races but intervened to break them up. Nehemiah says he found Jews who had married women of Ashdod, Ammon, and Moab, and says he "contended with them and cursed them and beat some of them and pulled out their hair, and made them take an oath in the name of God, saying, 'You shall not give your daughters to their sons, or take their daughters for your sons or yourselves.'"[34] Some scholars believe that the book of Ruth was written specifically to dispute

---

30 W. Gunther Plaut, in *The Torah, A Modern Commentary*, Union of American Hebrew Congregations, New York, 1981, p. 556.
31 Luke 14.26.
32 Mark 3.34, Matthew 12.49.
33 Luke 8.21.
34 Nehemiah 13.23–25.

this position. Ruth, a woman of Moab, marries a Jew who has moved with his mother and brother to her land. When the husband and his brother die, Ruth remains faithful to her mother-in-law, returning to Judah with her, marrying a relative of her husband, and bearing a child. In the narrative many of the usual biblical assumptions of the relative priority of male and female roles are reversed,[35] and Ruth, the foreign woman who ought to be despised, becomes a national heroine as the great-grandmother of King David.

It is true that these and other apparent contradictions may be subsumed within a larger theology or scheme of commentary and interpretation or may be explained in relation to the social context, but it is also true that, when we need such explanations to resolve contradictions, we are bringing the principle of authority from outside the particular text, even from outside the scriptures themselves, and relying on our own judgement. In this context we may remember that Martin Luther, whose life had been changed by Paul's theology of salvation by faith alone, was prepared to dismiss the letter of James as "straw."

Luther was not alone in applying his own principles of selection to a biblical text whose authority he did not perceive to be uniform. There are 613 commandments in the *Torah*, the definitive first five books of the Jewish bible, and Orthodox Jews consider them to be binding. However, they make exceptions for those commandments that relate to the ritual practice of the Jerusalem temple, since the temple was destroyed in 70 CE

---

35   See Aldina da Silva, "Ruth, plaidoyer en faveur de la femme," in *Studies in Religion/Sciences Religieuses*, vol. 27, no. 3, 1998.

and its ritual practice is no longer possible. Article VII[36] of the Anglican Thirty-nine Articles makes a parallel distinction: "Although the Law given from God by Moses, as touching Ceremonies and Rites, do not bind Christian men, nor the Civil precepts thereof ought of necessity to be received in any commonwealth; yet notwithstanding, no Christian man whatsoever is free from the obedience of the Commandments which are called Moral." The Article does not, however, provide a clear guide for the application of this distinction between ritual and civil matters on one hand, and moral matters on the other hand, as we shall see.

The chequered history of the charging of interest for loans of money or goods provides an example of confusion over the nature of Scripture. The Bible is quite explicit on the matter. Exodus 22.25 reads, "If you lend money to my people, to the poor among you, you shall not deal with them as a creditor; you shall not exact interest from them," and Deuteronomy 23.19 reads, "You shall not charge interest on loans to another Israelite, interest on money, interest on provisions, interest on anything that is lent. On loans to a foreigner you may charge interest, but on loans to another Israelite you may not charge interest." These commandments are clearly neither ceremonial nor civil in any legal or constitutional sense of the term. They are moral and touch directly on the integrity of relationships and the prevention of exploitation. Nor can they be dismissed by Christians as applying only to Jews, since almost all of Old Testament moral law was originally written solely for the Jewish people and was acquired by Christians along with the rest of the Jewish scriptures. Ezekiel includes the taking of

---

36   "Of the Old Testament."

advance or accrued interest in three lists of mortal sins, along with idolatry, defiling one's neighbour's wife, approaching a woman during her menstrual period, robbery, and oppression, and he never suggests that it is forbidden only within the national circle.[37]

During the early centuries of Christian history the spirit of these commandments against charging interest was enforced on clergy, and in the fourth century it began to be extended to lay people. Eventually the charging of interest was condemned, although the Fourth Lateran Council (1215) allowed Jews to lend money for a fee—an exception that gave them a special role in the financial structure of the medieval period and contributed to the resentment that fuelled persecution, pogroms and, eventually, the holocaust (see *The Merchant of Venice* for evidence). Many early leaders of the Reformation maintained the medieval church's condemnation of interest-taking, and it was still forbidden in England even as the Thirty-nine Articles were being written. But John Calvin had opened the door to interest in certain cases, and in England in 1571 the prohibition was lifted to allow for moderate charges of interest. Christians today may condemn excessive and exploitative interest as unjust, but do so on the basis of its injustice and not in obedience to a commandment that tormented Western business for nearly 1,000 years but is no longer regarded as binding. Today, business, personal finance, the real estate industry, and pension plans all depend on a reasonable interest on loans.

There are many other commandments, neither ceremonial nor civil in nature, in both the Jewish and Christian scriptures, that significant numbers of Christians have judged to be not

---

37 Ezekiel 18.5–13

binding. Some examples are the commandment to leave some unharvested produce in the fields for the poor to gather (Leviticus 19.9f and Deuteronomy 24.19–22), the commandment not to sow two kinds of seed in the same field or wear clothes made of two different materials (Leviticus 19.19),[38] the commandment not to be tattooed (Leviticus 19.28), the commandment to observe a sabbatical year and the jubilee year (Leviticus 25.1–12, the provision for parents to request the execution of a rebellious son (Deuteronomy 21.18–25), Jesus' apparent prohibition of divorce (Matthew 19.9, Mark 10.11–12, Luke 16.18), Paul's injunctions on women and men respectively covering and uncovering their heads while praying (1 Corinthians 11.1–16), Paul's requirements that women should not speak in church because it is "shameful," his insistence that they should be subordinate, and should consult their husbands on anything they do not understand (1 Corinthians 14.34f),[39] the requirement in 1 Timothy that women learn in silence and exercise no teaching authority (1 Timothy 2.10–11), the requirement in 1 Timothy that women not braid their hair or wear gold, pearls, or expensive clothes (1 Timothy 2.9), the requirement in 1 Timothy that a bishop be married only once (1 Timothy 3.2). Clearly a great many Christians do not recognize these

---

38 Some may consider this commandment to be ceremonial or ritual in nature simply because it is puzzling to us. However, some scholars believe that the Hebrew notion of evil is closely related to the mixing of things that do not belong naturally together. I once heard James Barr, then Regius Professor of Hebrew as Oxford, suggest that the *real* fall event in the Jewish scriptures may be the sexual union of the sons of God and the daughters of men (Genesis 6.1–8).

39 Some scholars believe 1 Corinthians 14.34–36 is a post-Pauline insertion into the text. In some manuscripts it appears after verse 40. It is, nevertheless, part of Holy Scripture as we have received it.

passages of Scripture as media "through which God communicates with us authoritatively," nor that they are the rule and ultimate standard of faith and practice.

There is another category of Scripture—the great narratives and stories—in which we might expect to find authority presented in the form of model or example. Certainly, there are many examples with which we may identify. We can imagine ourselves as Abraham being called into a new land and a new destiny. We can imagine ourselves as Moses at the burning bush, taking off his sandals in the holy place. We can imagine ourselves as Hebrews escaping from Egypt, or exiles going home from Babylon, or outcasts gathered by Jesus into the welcoming circle of a table of acceptance. We can imagine ourselves as Peter, terrified into denial. We can imagine ourselves as the Emmaus pilgrims when the bread is broken.

But there are stories in the Bible with which we cannot identify, unless we are perverse. There is the frightful story of the rape of Tamar by her half-brother Amnon, who first lustfully adored her and then, when he had forced her, loathed her and threw her out (2 Samuel 13). The only redeeming feature of the story is the heart-rending pathos of her anguish, which wafts to us on an acid breeze across the centuries and gives voice to many victims who have followed her.

There is the equally dreadful story of the destruction of the Amalekites because they resisted Israel's invasion of their land (1 Samuel 15). In a particularly vivid passage, the prophet Samuel hacks Agag, the Amalekite king, to pieces "before the Lord." It is true that the story could be used to reinforce obedience, because Saul, the Israelite king, failed to complete the task as commanded and consequently lost his throne. On the other hand, it has equally provided a potential model and example for every act of genocide and so-called "ethnic cleansing" committed by people under the influence of the Bible ever since.

Most people asked to identify David's gravest sin would probably respond with the story of his adultery with Bathsheba and his military murder of her husband, Uriah the Hittite (2 Samuel 11.2—12.25). The story meets our cultural need to save our sharpest disapproval for sexual sins, although readers of the time may have understood its central points of moral failure to have been David's appropriation of Uriah's property (Bathsheba) and his total lack of integrity towards a man who was not only a brave soldier but a foreigner, a stranger within the gates, and therefore under particular divine protection. Certainly God punished David for his sin to his great distress, in the form of the death of the child Bathsheba had conceived by him. But if God's disapproval is to be measured in terms of the death he inflicts in judgement, this sin pales in comparison to another event in David's life.

In 2 Samuel 24 and 1 Chronicles 21 we read that David committed a sin so grave (admittedly with a little prodding by God in one account and by Satan in the other) that God told him to choose between three years of famine, three months of devastation by an enemy, and three days of pestilence. David, in mental anguish, could not choose, so God elected pestilence and killed 70,000 people of Israel with a plague. What is this sin that is 70,000 times more serious than adultery and murder? David's sin was that he took a census and had the population of his nation counted. We are not told the reason why this was sinful. Perhaps the story reflects the transition from reliance on God for victory to the maintenance of an adequate army (the numbers reported were all of fighting men). Perhaps a census suggested that it was prudent to check up on God's promise to multiply the nation. We know only that David counted Israel and it was wrong.

Does this story have implications for us? Have we a solemn duty to resist our governments when they gather statistics? Is it a grave transgression to participate in opinion polls or to register for elections? Should we treat a military conscription as some form of blasphemy? Or do we give different weight to the stories of David and Bathsheba and David and the census? And, if so, why?

The truth is that we cannot treat the Bible as though it were an immutable deposit of tribal wisdom, although it contains wisdom. We cannot treat the Bible as a rational and coherent system of law, although it contains some laws that remain valuable and important. We cannot treat the Bible as an integrated system of philosophy, although it contains reflection of lasting brilliance. We cannot treat the Bible as great poetry, although it includes poetry of sublime sensitivity. And we cannot treat the Bible as an oracular communication from God to humanity, each part of which is equal to all the others and may be used in isolation from the rest to rule definitively on the moral problems of our own day.

We *can* treat the Bible as the collected literature of a people engaged in a great spiritual pilgrimage in response to their awareness of God as the power of salvation running through the universe. We can treat the Bible as the reflection of their profound intuition of the presence and purpose of God. In fact, what we see in the Bible is *their response* to that divine presence. We may not see the presence in the Bible, but the Bible may enable us to see the presence in our lives. The people of the Bible experienced God in the liberation of slaves, in the gift of land and identity, in the challenge of holiness expressed in responsible living in relation to God and neighbour, in judgement for oppression and callousness, in deliverance from exile, in hope for a new age, in the unveiling of a new order in which the accepted values of power and domination are reversed, in the demonstration of compassion, in the transforming power of the mutual acceptance of the unaccepted, in the victory of total self-giving. It is this experience, told as story, that did and can transfigure human life. The Bible communicates this experience, makes it available, but not legislatively or logically.

The Bible's medium of communication is symbol. This makes it close *in form* to the communication process of tribal cultures, which find expression in story and symbol, but more distant from them *in content* because the Bible is always open to liberation, transformation, and change. The Bible is closer to town life culture *in content* because they both share a sense of the importance of history, but more distant *in form* because it is not a legal or rational instrument.

The Bible is symbolic. But in order to grasp what this means, we will have to explore the word *symbol*.

3
The Bible as Symbol

HUMAN COMMUNICATION DEPENDS on symbols, some of them simple and some complex, some of them superficial and some profound. Our languages are symbol systems. When, as an English-speaker, I use my lips to make the noise we associate with the letter *m*, and follow it immediately by a long *e*, I get the sound that we associate with the word *me*. That sound, which is not in itself any part of the person I know as myself, functions within the agreed consensus of our language system as a symbol to inform others that I am talking about myself. Languages consist of thousands of such sounds used in thousands of combinations to share information and ideas.

My encyclopaedia defines a symbol as, "[a] sign representing something that has an independent existence."[40] It is a matter of one thing standing for another—sounds for objects,

---

40 *The Canadian Encyclopedia Plus* Copyright © 1995 by McClelland & Stewart Inc. *The Columbia Encyclopedia*, Fifth Edition Copyright © 1993 by Columbia University Press. CD-ROM edition.

squiggles on a page for spoken words, letters for the chemical elements of the earth.[41]

There are layers and levels of complexity and profundity in the realm of symbolism. Beyond the symbols that have no inherent significance of their own and that function simply as tags to identify external objects (I call them "low" symbols), there are "high" symbols, which carry some of their original meaning into another set of circumstances. Fire, for instance, may purify a forest of dead wood. If it is used in conjunction with prayer, as in some oriental religions, it suggests that the ritual is a supplication for purification. Water, also an agent of cleansing, may be used to wash parts of the body as a preparation for prayer (as in Islam). Personal cleanliness symbolizes spiritual cleanliness and preparation for encounter with the divine. The gifts of the magi in Matthew's account of Jesus' birth[42] are symbolic, as the hymn, "We three kings of orient are" labours to illustrate.

The use of metaphor provides a particularly rich example of symbolism. Again and again we say one thing to expand and interpret another. "You are my sunshine," sang the Andrews Sisters in a popular song of long ago. No heavy-handed exegesis is needed to unpack this symbolism: we immediately

---

41 I have skirted away from the distinction between sign and symbol that understands the former as a pointer towards a reality that is somewhere else (like a sign that says, "Saskatoon 15 km") and the latter as a means of participation in a present reality (like a handshake or a kiss as participation in, and expression of, friendship and affection). The subject of this chapter is symbolism. Usually when people say, "Only a symbol," they are really talking about signs. A symbol is a present reality, held in tension with another reality to which it provides access.

42 Matthew 2.1–12

recall the radiance that the experience of being in love brings with it.

Christian prayer and hymnody abound in the symbolism of metaphor. The psalms are full of it. God is called shepherd, rock, shield, king, refuge, fortress, dwelling place, father. God is actually none of these things; rather, they are realities in human experience through which we have some intuition of what God is like. From time to time we have to pinch ourselves to remember that these metaphors are *not* God, an exercise prompted to our great benefit by theologically-informed feminist critique in recent years. We had settled so easily into using a number of masculine metaphors for God that we half-consciously assumed that God was male. From time to time our metaphors must be reviewed, renewed, and expanded.

On the other hand, at an early point in the feminist critique of masculine metaphors it became fashionable to cut out offending verbal images and simply replace them with the word *God*. In many places, "Glory to God in the highest, and peace to his people on earth," became "Glory to God in the highest, and peace to *God's* people on earth." As this practice expanded, the word *God* began to lose meaning because the meaning had been suggested by the metaphors, which now were gone. This had a curious double effect. On one hand, the atmosphere of some hymns and prayers became somewhat atheistic: if God couldn't be understood in terms of anything in particular, was God anything at all? At the same time our unmodified use of the word God seemed to suggest that it somehow grasped and encompassed God, that *God* was in fact the divine name. In this context I came to understand the Jewish prohibition against reciting the sacred name: if the identity and power of the infinite are in the name, then it would be arrogance to use it. It is not surprising that some Orthodox Jews not only avoid the prohibited name of God but also modify the names that are commonly substituted for it (*Adonai* and *Elohim*), and write G-d and L-rd in English to avoid any appearance of taking the holy for granted.[43]

The higher symbols, whether secular or religious, carry with them the nature and power of that which they symbolize. They are performative, doing what they suggest. In some cultures it has been customary to give the children of a family a key to the house on a particular birthday. They may, in fact, have been letting themselves in with a key for some time, but the gift of a key on a particular anniversary and in the context of a family celebration confers a deeper recognition of independence. When a man places a ring on a woman's finger and says, "With this ring I thee wed," his action and her acceptance of it change the direction of their lives. The ring and the action are symbolic and the performance achieves what is symbolized.

In Christian controversies over the relationship of the bread and wine of the eucharist to the body and blood of Christ, it became customary in some circles to denigrate those whose interpretation of the sacrament was perceived to be "only symbolic." There is, in fact, no such thing as "only symbolic." Symbols are the way we communicate (itself an important word in discussions about the eucharist). As Paul Tillich observed, there is nothing we can say about God that is not symbolic, (except, he added elusively, the statement that there is nothing

---

43   W. Gunther Plaut, in *The Torah, A Modern Commentary*, Union of American Hebrew Congregations, New York, 1981, p. 543.

we can say about God that is not symbolic.)[44] We speak of God through the finite things around us insofar as they are rooted in God; at the same time, they remain inadequate because there is no absolute but the Absolute. If we were able to say anything about God *as God is*, our words would become absolute and God would not be One. The closest we can get, apart from symbols, is silence—*not* speaking—and the offering of a cup of cold water (a gesture of compassionate responsibility) to one who needs it.

Perhaps the highest symbolism, the symbolism we use in the most sensitive areas of theology, involves saying that one thing is another without ceasing to be itself. We say, "*This* is *that*, but still *this*.*" It may be helpful to illustrate this level of symbolism from a non-Christian context before exploring it in our own tradition.

In the ritual of the Passover Seder, when the first cup of wine has been drunk and the preliminary ceremonies have been completed, the leader begins the Passover story (the *Haggadah*) by lifting the plate of unleavened bread (*matzot*) and saying, "This is the bread of affliction which Israel ate in the land of Egypt."[45] Of course everyone at the table knows that the *matzot* were bought at Cohen's Delicatessen a couple of days ago, but they also know that the *matzot* are the means by which they participate in the bitter slavery of their ancestors and identify with the oppressed hungry of succeeding centuries and their

---

44   Paul Tillich, *Systematic Theology*, vol. 2, The University of Chicago Press, 1957, p. 9.
45   Rabbi Leon Klenicki, ed., *The Passover Celebration*, The Anti-Defamation League of B'nai B'rith and The Liturgy Training Program of the Archdiocese of Chicago, 1980, p. 25.

own time. Through the *matzot* they share in that history and thereby open themselves to hope.

The centre of Christian theology is the doctrine of the Incarnation, which teaches that Jesus of Nazareth, in his person, teaching, ministry, and victory, is the unique revelation of God and means of participation in God.[46] Behind this somewhat dry and rational statement lies a symbolic understanding of Jesus, which we may glimpse in the pages of the New Testament, especially in the synoptic gospels. It is simply: this man is God, but still man.

We are so used to a presentation of Jesus from the point of view of eternity (the eternal Word coming down) that we tend to lose sight of Jesus from the point of view of history (the man in whom others discovered God). The hymns, prayers, and piety we encountered from earliest childhood (if we were brought up in Christian households) present Jesus as deity. But the sequence was reversed for his disciples. They met him as a remarkable teacher, a healer, a man of prayer, one who confronted and challenged the values and standards of his society (and especially those that contributed to oppression), who taught that God's holy reign (as opposed to Caesar's military occupation) had already begun and was around them waiting to be seized. Gradually it dawned on them that in and through his humanity they could glimpse God. He was, in the highest sense of the word, the symbol of God.

There is nothing wrong with a theology of Jesus based on the point of view of eternity. It appears at various points in the

---

46   See Article II of the Thirty-nine Articles, "Of the Word or Son of God, which was made very Man," for a more formal statement of Incarnational orthodoxy.

Christian scriptures and is the model of John's gospel. But there is something seriously wrong if it is the only theology you have. The controversies, often bitter and sometimes violent, of the first five centuries of Christian history witness powerfully to the need for balance in symbolic statements. "This is that, and *not* still this," is full of pitfalls.

In the first quarter of the fourth century an Alexandrian priest named Arius attempted to explain the relationship of Jesus to the Godhead. Arius took for granted a theology of Jesus based on the point of view of eternity. Essentially, he taught that the eternal Word, incarnate in Jesus, was created before the worlds. This made Jesus almost divine, but not quite. Arianism caused a great controversy and in order to keep the peace of the empire, the emperor Constantine assembled a Council at Nicaea, which ruled that the eternal Word was "eternally begotten of the Father," and "of one being with the Father." The theological statement produced by the Council became the basis of a creed.

A few years later, near Antioch, the bishop of Laodicea, a man named Apollinarius, veered in the opposite direction. In order to affirm the divinity of Jesus he taught that the divine Word, of one being with the Father, had taken the place of Jesus' human spirit or mind. This made Jesus fully God, but only somewhat human. The Council of Constantinople condemned this teaching. Popular history, which is now questioned, attributes to this Council the completion of the creed that was started at Nicaea.

And then the pursuit of the right definition took the opposite tack again. Early in the next century a man named Nestorius, the bishop of Constantinople, taught that Jesus was "two persons," one human and one divine, inseparably united. He refused to use the title *Theotokos* (literally *God-bearer*, but usually translated *Mother of God*) for Mary, because Jesus was the Father's son as God, but Mary's son as a human. The Council of Ephesus rejected this teaching.

A fourth venture was made by a monk named Eutyches, who revived the teachings of Apollinarius with a new twist. He taught that Jesus had one divine nature in which his human nature had been absorbed like a drop of water in the ocean. (This teaching is called *Monophysitism*, from the Greek for *one nature*.) The result was that Jesus is God but no longer man. The Council of Chalcedon ruled that the Christ has two natures, one divine and one human, and that they exist inseparably in one person.

This tortuous process (and it was not fully over) had an unfortunate effect on Christian theology. It carried theology out of the realm of symbolism into the world of speculation, out of the realm of story and icon into the world of Greek philosophy. The wonderful fluidity of the paradox of symbolism (*this* is *that*, but still *this*) is replaced by grammar and syntax and a rational process. Unfortunately, the decrees of the councils do not solve the problem by providing an adequate and satisfying description of the relationship between Jesus and God. At best they fence the area, like the police at the site of an accident, preventing trespass on a critical but ineffable area of Christian reflection.

We cannot turn back the clock and pretend the conciliar period in Christian history never happened. The Nicene Creed is there to remind us. We can, however, cultivate a sensitivity to symbolism and try to make sure that we hold onto both ends of the symbolic structure at the same time. I do not wish to deny the pronouncements of the orthodox councils, but I would like to get behind them to the biblical image of Jesus as the symbol of God, the man whose followers so experienced him that they recognized him as God, but still man.

Many Christians today are really followers of Apollinarius and Eutyches: they suppress Jesus' humanity and think of him mostly as God. (Many more do not think this way but keep their ideas to themselves because they believe it is the official doctrine.) The effect of this is to treat him as *a* god, for if you say, "This man is God," and fail to go on to say, "and yet he is still man," you have elevated the appearance of finite humanity to absolute status. It is possible to treat Jesus as an idol if you think of what looked like his humanity as only a platform for deification.

Something similar to this happened to our understanding of the eucharist. It is clear from the Christian scriptures that meals were central to the ministry of Jesus. He ate and drank with sinners and outcasts. He ate in the house of Simon the leper. He ate with Simon the Pharisee. He used banquets and dinners in his parables. The account of the feeding of the multitude appears more often than any other in the Christian scriptures. Some of the post-resurrection stories are meal-centred—appearing to the disciples while they were at table, blessing the bread at Emmaus, eating fish in the upper room, the lakeside barbecue at Galilee. Meals must have been symbolic for Jesus of what he called the kingdom of God. Sharing food and drink together is to be in the kingdom of God, although we are still here.

The accounts of what Jesus did at the last supper must be seen within this context and against this background. For Jesus, all meals seem to have been symbols of God's kingdom, but surely none more than a meal with his closest followers at the Passover season, when the air was full of tribal memories of liberation from oppression and the establishment of a nation whose holiness was rooted in mutual responsibility and care. Jesus knew that his mission to give new meaning to that old vision was in tatters, that his challenge of conventional values, economic exploitation, and a conservative religious system that shored up the status quo had attracted the hostility of several institutions of power. Knowing he was unlikely to survive the week, he made the basic commodities of a Mediterranean table the symbols of his continuing presence in the community of those who only half understood him, if that. This bread is his body, yet still bread; this cup is his blood, but still wine.

Unfortunately, in the course of time some Christians could not bear to live with the paradox of the Lord's table. They had difficulty with the words, "yet still bread ... but still wine," just as they had difficulty with the words, "but still man," when they discussed the nature and person of Jesus as the Christ. Words like *symbol* and *figure* were used, but the tone of description was increasingly literal. The matter came to a head in the eleventh century, when a scholar named Berengar was accused of regarding the sacrament, "not as the real body and real blood of Christ but a kind of figure and likeness," and for holding that the body of Christ is in the sacrament "in such a way that the nature and essence of the bread and wine are not changed."[47]

Berengar was excommunicated. Later he was pressed to burn his writings and to subscribe to a statement that included the words, "the bread and wine which are placed on the altar are after consecration not only a Sacrament but also the real body and blood of our Lord Jesus Christ, and that with the senses (*sensualiter*) not only by way of Sacrament but in reality (*non solum sacramento sed in veritate*) these are held and

---

47   Darwell Stone, *A History of the Doctrine of the Holy Eucharist*, Longmans, Green, & Co., London, 1909, vol. 1, pp. 244ff.

broken by the hands of the priests and are crushed by the teeth of the faithful."[48]

This literalist point of view found expression in the theology of *Transubstantiation*, that is, the conversion of the reality of the bread and wine into the reality of the body and blood of Christ, so that nothing of the bread and wine remains except their appearances. This doctrine was defined as official teaching of the church by the Fourth Lateran Council in 1215. It was roundly denounced by Anglican Reformers in Article XXVIII.[49]

> Transubstantiation (or the change of the substance of Bread and Wine) in the Supper of the Lord, cannot be proved by holy Writ; but is repugnant to the plain words of Scripture, overthroweth the nature of a Sacrament, and hath given occasion to many superstitions.

The important point for our present purpose is the clause, "overthroweth the nature of a Sacrament," for a sacrament as a high form of symbol must necessarily have the two dimensions we have identified. Transubstantiation says, "This is that," but it categorically denies, "but still this." It effectively carries the Apollinarian and Monophysite heresies from the earlier conversation about the nature of Jesus as the Christ into the medieval theology of the sacraments.

It is possible to treat the Bible in exactly the way earlier generations of Christians treated the person of Jesus and the sacrament of the Lord's Supper. It is possible to deny the

---

48 Stone, ibid.
49 "Of the Lord's Supper."

human, this-world dimension of the Bible and with the same devastating results. Our protection against this temptation to idolatry is to understand the Bible as symbolic. This exploration is the next step in this pilgrimage.

4
Finding the Word in the Words

IF WE APPROACH Jesus from the point of view of ordinary human experience, we see first of all a man. If we approach the bread of the eucharist from the point of view of ordinary human experience, we see first of all flour and water, and perhaps yeast, which have been kneaded together and baked. If we approach the wine of the eucharist from the point of view of ordinary human experience, we see first of all grape juice, which has been allowed to ferment. Later, as we understand this man and these things, we may see much more, but this is what we first see.

If we approach the Bible from the point of view of ordinary human experience, we see first of all the collected religious literature of a great faith tradition. As with Jesus, and the bread and wine of the eucharist, we may in the course of time come to recognize the Bible as much more than this. It may provide us with vision, insight, challenge, comfort, hope, conviction, joy, renewal—everything we mean by the word *faith*. But it is, first of all, a collection of writings put down on vellum or parchment or papyrus by people.

The very untidiness of this collection of writings witnesses to its human dimension. There is some variation in its content from one sub-community of faith to another. It has had a complex history of transmission in a large number of varying manuscripts. It is also, from the point of view of ordinary human experience, an uneven collection, witnessing by variations in style, method, and subject to the hands of many writers and editors over more than a millennium. Stuart Blanch, former Archbishop of York, has illustrated the diversity of the biblical material:

> Imagine 'Gibbons's Decline and Fall of the Roman Empire, the collected poems of T.S. Eliot, the Textus Roffensis, Hamlet, Robinson's Honest to God, the Canterbury Tales, Holinshed's Chronicles, the Cathedral Statutes of Rochester, Hymns Ancient and Modern (Revised), Bonhoeffer's Letters and Papers from Prison, Hammersjkold's Markings, The thoughts of Chairman Mao, Pilgrim's Progress, the Sixteen Satires of Juvenal and the Book of Kells' deprived of indications of date and authorship, all printed in the same format and bound together as a single volume; the analogy suggests that it is natural that the library comprising the Jewish and Christian Scriptures manifests such diversity of viewpoint.[50]

As a vast collection of religious literature, assembled over a long period of time, the Bible not unexpectedly contains some material that is specific to certain moments in its history. Christians generally ignore the ritual commandments of the Jewish scriptures—as Article VII of the Anglican Thirty-nine Articles testifies. Many Christians ignore Paul's edicts on the role,

---

50 Quoted in Richard Holloway, *Godless Morality*, Canongate, London, 1999, p. 82.

decorum, and dress of women in the Christian assembly. As we have seen, Christians do not regard the genocide of the Amalekites as a model for contemporary political behaviour. The legal arrangements for slavery in Exodus 21 and the general indifference to slavery that we find in the Christian scriptures are not regarded by most Christians as consistent with the commandment to love one's neighbour as oneself. The hymn in praise of murdering Babylonian children in the final verses of Psalm 137 is not taken as a moral standard. And so on. There are byways and false starts. The argument in Article VI, that "it is not lawful for the Church to ordain anything that is contrary to God's Word written," is simply not accepted in practice as an inflexible standard of biblical interpretation.

On the other hand, the Bible is tied together by great themes that appear and reappear in its pages. They are the themes of liberation of the oppressed, empowerment of the alienated, the gift of community, judgement for those who practise idolatry and exploitation, exile, return, forgiveness, wholeness, the transforming power of self-giving, hope. They are the themes of salvation. They are themes that, for Christians, culminate in the vision of the reign of God proclaimed and enacted by Jesus in both his failure and his victory, a divine commonwealth already present for those who will accept and lay hold of it. This vision, which is the subject of the Bible, is God's word to us

We do not say that the Bible is the *words* of God: that would absolutize each verbal unit in the text, presumably in its original language. We say that the Bible is the word of God, which is a symbolic statement. We mean that this collected literature of our faith tradition is our intimation of the purpose of God as the power of salvation running through the universe, and *yet is still the collected literature of our faith tradition*. These stories and hymns, this wisdom and counsel, they are the outward and visible sign of the pilgrimage of a community of which we are part. They make the whole tradition available to us, so that we may find our path in their model.[51]

When we recognize the symbolic quality of the statement, "the Bible is the word of God," we are not denigrating the Bible; we are looking into the profundity of its meaning. To claim that the Bible is the word of God in some absolute sense that demands the reconciliation of every apparent contradiction, as well as rigid obedience to every enforceable commandment, is to apply the error of transubstantion to the scriptures. So is the suggestion that God, "communicates with us authoritatively through the Holy Scriptures of the Old and New Testaments," if this means that the element of human history has been removed (like the *breadness* of bread) to make way for a stream of information unconditioned by the process of time and experience. This is the effect of saying that this collection of religious literature is the word of God without affirming that it is still a collection of religious literature.

People in some tribal cultures may find it difficult to deal with the extent to which the Bible has been conditioned by the various moments in history in which it was produced, because history is sometimes not their primary point of reference. This does not mean that people in such cultures are stupid about past events, but only that the inherited stories of their origins and the patterns of traditional ways are more important. It has not been hard for people with a strong sense of myth to appro-

---

51　See Daniel Shin, "Some Light from Origen: Scripture as Sacrament," in *Worship*, September 1999, vol. 73, no. 5, pp. 399–424, published since the above was written.

priate the Bible as part of their mythic heritage.[52] Myth, and the rituals and taboos that accompany it, is beyond challenge and resistant to change. It is the wisdom of the elders. It is bedrock. Where biblical injunctions accord with the inherited assumptions of a culture, they reinforce this absolute quality.

Cultures with a town style have found it easy to lift the Bible out of its historical contexts and incorporate it into a system of law in their own contexts. It may be used to illustrate and defend conclusions reached by a speculative process. Or it may, as in the hands of some of the leaders of the Reformation, become a replacement for the tradition and canon law of the church.

It is important to recall at this point the resistance of Anglican teaching to treatment of the Bible as a code. Article VI states simply that, "Holy Scripture containeth all things necessary to salvation: so that whatsoever is not read therein, nor may be proved thereby, is not to be required of any man, that it should be believed as an article of the Faith, or be thought requisite or necessary to salvation." The ordination rite that was attached to the first Book of Common Prayer of 1549, and that became normative in the Prayer Book tradition, requires the bishop to ask a candidate for priesthood,

> Be you persuaded that the holy Scriptures contain all
> doctrine required of necessity for eternal salvation,
> through faith in Jesu Christ? And are you determined
> with the said scriptures to instruct the people com-

---

52 I use the word *myth* not in reference to untrue stories but to describe stories that contain for a culture the ultimate truth of their reality in time and place.

mitted to your charge, and to teach nothing, as required of necessity, to eternal salvation, but that you shall be persuaded may be concluded and proved by the scripture?"[53]

This interpretation of the place of Scripture drives a very careful and typically Anglican *via media* between pre-Reformation reliance on tradition functioning in independence of Scripture and Protestant biblicism. Richard Hooker, who might be described as the father of Anglican theology, expanded on this point.

Two opinions therefore there are concerning sufficiency of Holy Scripture, each extremely opposite unto the other, and both repugnant unto truth. The schools of Rome teach Scripture to be so unsufficient, as if, except traditions were added, it did not contain all revealed and supernatural truth, which absolutely is necessary for the children of men in this life to know that they may in the next be saved. Others justly condemning this opinion grow likewise unto a dangerous extremity, as if Scripture did not only contain all things in that kind necessary, but all things simply, and in such sort that to do any thing according to any other law were not only unnecessary but even opposite unto salvation, unlawful and sinful. Whatsoever is spoken of God or things appertaining to God otherwise than as the truth is, though it seem an honour it

_____.

53 *The First and Second Prayer Books of Edward VI*, Dent, Everyman's Library, London, 1968, p. 309. Language modernized.

is an injury. And as incredible praises given unto men do often abate and impair the credit of their deserved commendation; so we must likewise take great heed, lest in attributing unto Scripture more than it can have, the incredibility of that do cause even those things which indeed it hath most abundantly to be less reverently esteemed.[54]

How do we judge between one part of Scripture and another? How do we decide which portions to emphasize and which to leave aside? The church, which is a living community engaged in active dialogue, tends to judge the relative importance of individual sections of the Bible by their relationship to the thematic whole. How does any particular passage of Scripture relate to that great sweep of grace that runs from the liberation of an

---

54 Richard Hooker, "Of the Laws of Ecclesiastical Polity," II.viii.7, in Keble, ed., et al, *The Works of That Learned and Judicious Divine Mr. Richard Hooker*, Clarendon Press, Oxford, 1888, p. 335f. I offer the following paraphrase of Hooker's elegant but dense style. "There are two opinions about the sufficiency of Holy Scripture, each of them opposed to the other and both of them contrary to truth. [Roman] Catholic theological opinion teaches that Scripture is so insufficient in itself that without the addition of the [church's] traditions, it would not contain that revealed and supernatural truth that is necessary for people to know in this life if they are going to be saved in the next life. Others who properly condemn this opinion go to the opposite extreme and teach that Scripture not only contains that truth that is necessary for salvation but is the only truth there is, so that to do anything that Scripture does not require would not only be unnecessary but would be sinful and unlawful and in conflict with the hope of salvation. But it is a fact that anything you say about God or things related to God other than what is true is actually an injury even if it is intended to be an honour. Just as exaggerated praises may actually undermine the reputation of those to whom they are offered, so we must be careful not to attribute to Scripture more status than it can enjoy lest our exaggeration of its importance results in people treating it irreverently."

enslaved people, through their discovery of God's holiness and justice and the vision of a realm of kindness and peace, into Jesus' proclamation and embodiment of God's commonwealth of forgiveness, self-giving, and wholeness? It is not for nothing that one of the most frequent morning hymns across Christianity has been the Song of Zechariah.

> Blessed are you, Lord, the God of Israel,
> you have come to your people and set them free.
> You have raised up for us a mighty Saviour,
> born of the house of your servant, David ....
> In the tender compassion of our God
> the dawn from on high shall break upon us,
> To shine on those who dwell in darkness
>   and the shadow of death,
> and to guide our feet into the way of peace

One of the ways we judge between one part of Scripture and another is by the creation of lectionaries or schemes for public reading. Much of the Bible was actually created for public reading, and even more of it was selected because it was considered to be suitable for proclamation in the assembly of worshippers. However, most Christian churches today follow lectionary schemes that do not attempt to include every verse of every biblical book. There is consequently a "canon within the canon," an identification of texts that together represent the central movement of the tradition. Deciding what to read and proclaim is an ongoing process because we do not simply submit to the Bible, we *engage* with it.

For Christians there is another method to weigh the importance of any biblical injunction, and it is attributed to Jesus himself. Someone asked Jesus to identify the "first" commandment of the 613 precepts of the law—presumably the commandment by which the others would be interpreted, and perhaps below which they would be ranked. Jesus replied with *two* commandments: "Hear, O Israel, the Lord our God, the Lord is one; you shall love the Lord your God with all your heart, with all your soul, with all your mind, and with all your strength," (Deuteronomy 6.4–5) and "You shall love your neighbour as yourself." (Leviticus 19.18) And he added, "There is no other commandment greater than these."[55] Every law, every prescription, must be judged against this background.

Jesus' ambivalent attitude to the legal tradition of his religion begins to become clearer at this point. On one hand, we are told by Matthew that Jesus said he had come to fulfil, not abolish, the law.[56] On the other hand, on such matters as strict Sabbath observance, family discipline, and ritual purity we know that he skated around the law as many others in his community understood it. How could he identify with the law and proclaim a gospel that appeared to subvert it at the same time? This tension has led some Christians to set law and gospel against each other, as though they were not only alternatives but opposites.

Jesus, as a first-century Jew, accepted the law as agenda, but went beyond that point. The law described the territory in which the struggle for goodness took place, but it did not exhaust it. The law was about *cases*, and Jesus' interpretation of the double commandment to love God and neighbour introduced the element of *people* and their well-being. Care for the sick and the satisfaction of hunger could take precedence over Sabbath observance. Personal integrity could take precedence over

---

55   Mark 12.28–31.
56   Matthew 5.17.

submission to an oppressive family system. Jesus challenged law when it was treated as an abstract system that applied theory to actions; when there was a conflict between that process and the affirmation and wholeness of people, he chose the latter.[57]

My suggestion that we use the great salvation themes of the Bible as the standard for the weight that we attach to individual passages of Scripture might come under the post-modern critique of *metanarratives* (stories we tell and general theories we expound about the nature and destiny of humanity and the direction of history[58]) if it were not for Jesus' pragmatic attention to people in their contexts. Jesus actually anticipates the culture of the secular city. He challenged the traditional law permitting divorce in order to provide greater protection for women who would otherwise have been abandoned. Thus he provided a model that has allowed us to challenge the rigorous and inflexible prohibition of divorce in order to provide relief to men and women whose marriages have become prisons of contempt or abuse. His rejection of divorce in one context allows us to permit divorce in another. The circumstances are different, but the principle of love (*agape* = commitment to compassion and responsibility) of God and neighbour is the constant factor.

This brings us to the application of the authority of Holy Scripture today.

---

57 It is important to note that other Jews held the positions attributed to Jesus and that he did not stand alone against the whole of Judaism. His conflict on matters of law was with those who practised a narrow interpretation. There is, for instance, a rabbinic principle that the law does not take precedence over human need. However, I suspect that just as Christians often fall short of their goal, so Jews have not always realized the highest ideals of their tradition. In any case, the principle that the law does not take precedence over human need seems to have been exactly the point that Jesus frequently tried to make.

58 See Adam, op. cit., p. 16ff. Adam notes that there is no single metanarrative in the Bible.

5
Homosexuality
and the Living Tradition

Now, let's review.

We can't claim any particular passage of the Bible as authoritative if it doesn't fit in with the prevailing and underlying pattern of the whole, with what Hooker called, "the main drift."[59]

We can't claim the Bible as a lawbook, composed of regulations that have to be enforced.

We can't claim that the Bible is consistent throughout, reflecting only a single point of view.

We can't claim that the Bible is a supernatural communication in which the human element only appears to be present.

We *can* claim the Bible as the outward and visible sign of a living community's experience of God as the power of salvation

---

59 "The main drift of the whole New Testament is that which St. John setteth down as the purpose of his own history; 'These things are written, that ye might believe that Jesus is Christ the Son of God, and that in believing ye might have life through his name.' The drift of the Old that which the Apostle mentioneth to Timothy, 'The Holy Scriptures are able to make thee wise unto salvation.' So that the general end both of Old and New is one ..." *Eccl. Pol.*, I.xiv.4.

over a long period of time. We *can* claim it as the corporate expression of the hope and faith that unites the people of the book, in spite of all the differences in language, race, piety and interpretation that separate them. We *can* claim it as the diary of a great pilgrimage that still goes on, in which we, too, are engaged

In this pilgrimage the gift of the Holy Spirit is the process of our own recognition of God as the power of salvation in a pattern that parallels and is informed by what we read in the Bible. If we think of the Jewish-Christian faith tradition as a great river, then the Bible is its chart. The river begins in small and often primitive tributaries; it moves sometimes quickly and sometimes slowly through the varying landscapes of history, with backwaters, undertows, eddies, even swamps along the shore-line, but always with a strong central current that carries it along. That central current is the story of liberation for slaves, justice for the exploited, judgement for oppressors; it is the story of steadfast, self-giving love (call it caring and compassion) as the most powerful motive force in human development; it is the story of responsibility to God and neighbour; it is the story of a kingdom of nobodies discovering that the ordinary values of self-interest and self-service can be turned upside-down; it is the story of a man who risked his life to pull all of this together in a movement that still goes on. And the Bible is the map of this river. All the backwaters, undertows, eddies, and swamps are there on the chart because they are part of the story. But the central current, "the main drift," is what really matters.

We can recognize that the Lambeth resolution that affirms that "God communicates with us authoritatively through the Holy Scriptures of the Old and New Testaments" has to be interpreted in the most guarded and reserved way. If it means that we glimpse the liberating and saving work of God through the narratives and reflections of the Bible, as its main drift, well and good. And if it means that we then have to discover what this glimpse means in our time and place, even better. But if it means that the Bible is a manual for our unconsidered application to every situation, then we know that we are in the presence of idolatry.

We can recognize that the Lambeth resolution that "upholds faithfulness in marriage between a man and a woman in lifelong union, and believes that abstinence is right for those who are not called to marriage," and affirms this " in view of the teaching of Scripture," needs to be treated with the utmost wariness. The Bible does not have a single teaching on marriage. Parts of the Jewish Scriptures testify to the acceptability of polygamy. Later parts celebrate monogamy, [60] but in a context that still tolerates the divorce of a woman by a man, but not vice versa. Jesus seems to be very positive about marriage,[61] and the church has used the story of his presence at the wedding in Cana of Galilee in its marriage rites for centuries. Paul, on the other hand, regarded marriage as a sort of last resort for those who would otherwise be "aflame with passion."[62] As we have already seen, Paul teaches the subordination of wives to their husbands,[63] and the author of the letter to the Ephesians said they should be subject to their husbands as the church is subject to Christ.[64] The Bible reflects a number of models of marriage, some of them simply not acceptable to devout Christian people now.

---

60 Ecclesiastes 9.9.
61 Matthew 19.5 and Mark 10.7.
62 1 Corinthians 7.9.
63 1 Corinthians 11.3–16, 14.34f
64 Ephesians 5.22ff.

Christian cultures today do not have a single model of marriage. In some societies marriage is treated as a component within the extended family, while in others it is understood to be the point at which an independent family unit is established. Some societies practise arranged marriage, while others insist on the absolute right of individuals to make their own choice of partners without the intervention of any third party. There is reason to believe that monogamy has not yet found universal acceptance throughout the Christian world. Certainly among Western Christians the practice of living together outside of marriage is not universally regarded as immoral or sinful, and many people in such relationships are active and committed members of Christian congregations. Neither the Bible nor Christian practice leaves the Lambeth resolution unchallenged.

Further, when we examine marriage from the point of view of Jesus' reversal of ordinary values, is it likely that he would have embraced a simplistic application of marriage law? In John's story of the Samaritan woman at the well, there is evidence that Jesus recognized her marital irregularities, but none whatever that he told her to amend them in accordance with some preconceived code. He accepted her, and told her about inner resources of which she had not been aware.

Tribal culture imposes the marital traditions that have developed within its own system. Town life culture imposes a legal formula, whether it is Paul's "last resort," or the complicated process of canon and civil law. Both suggest a "starting gun" approach to the marriage rite: relationships are defined one way before the gun is fired and in a very different way once the race has begun, as though the people involved and their commitment to each other were less important than the rules of the race. This approach is not consistent with Jesus' condemnation of mere legalism: "This people honours me with their lips, but their hearts are far from me; in vain do they worship me, teaching human precepts as doctrines."[65] There are people who live together without formal vows, whose style of relationship is exemplary. And there are people who live in marriages that are abusive—verbally, psychologically, and physically. There are people in loving and responsible relationships today who are afraid to embrace the formalities of marriage for fear it would destroy their God-given love—so trivialized is marriage in some corners of our culture, and so exaggerated the expectations laid upon it in others.[66] Does the Lambeth Conference stand in favour of marriage as an institution, no matter how trivial or misleading, and against responsible relationships unless they have the hallmark of respectability?

Perhaps we can begin to recognize that the Lambeth resolutions that reject homosexual practice as incompatible with Scripture, and cannot advise the legitimizing or blessing of same-sex unions or ordaining those involved in same-gender unions, must be treated with great care. There are, it is true, several passages of Scripture that condemn sexual relations between men, but there are many other equally forceful and prescriptive passages of Scripture to which we pay no attention whatever. Why have these texts been selected for enforcement? Is it pos-

---

65 Matthew 15.8f.
66 This point is captured brilliantly in the film *Four Weddings and a Funeral*, in which the only wedding with any hope of initiating a lasting marriage relationship is one in which the partners paradoxically commit themselves to one another while rejecting vows, and the only alliance to have reached the depth of true marriage is a gay relationship that is poignantly terminated by the death of one of the partners.

sible that we bring our own prejudices to Scripture and find there the condemnations we require? Do societies where traditional styles of marriage may have emphasized the concerns of families, as much or more than individuals, bring an understandable (but perhaps regrettable) conviction that homosexuality is fundamentally antisocial? Do the rest of us bring distaste for what we do not understand and find it reinforced by Scripture that we have not begun to examine in its own social context? Let us face the fact that we are all selective in our use of Scripture. It is vital that we be aware of the principles on which we base our selection. It is my conviction that those principles properly relate to the Bible's central current of liberation, justice, forgiveness, and the realization of God's reign in care, compassion, mutual responsibility, and self-giving.

If Jesus could challenge the Ten Commandments on the law of filial piety and relax them on the law of Sabbath observance, if he could confront his religion's traditional rules on divorce in the interest of protecting the vulnerable, if early Christians could question biblical indifference to the moral issues of slavery, if renaissance Christians could change the biblical and early Christian condemnation of usury—if we can do all these things and more, can we stop treating a handful of biblical statements on homosexuality, which sound like they were really written to condemn random and promiscuous encounters, as though they addressed all forms of homosexual relationships for all places and for all times?

What is homosexuality? Those who find it intolerable describe it in terms of "preference" or "choice," in order to emphasize an implicit moral culpability. More than one gay person has said to me, "Who would choose???" A more sober analysis by a clinical psychologist proposes that one can do no more than suggest that homosexuality describes those people who discover that when they fall in love it happens to be with a person of the same sex. It is not a choice, but a fact.[67] Can we encourage these people to give thanks for such love, and to commit themselves to a faithful relationship?

I think one of the reasons some heterosexual people have difficulty accepting a change in the official status of homosexual people in the church is that they approach the subject from the perspective of imagination rather than reason, and from emotional involvement rather than reflective detachment. What would it be like, they ask themselves, if we knew our parish priest was gay or lesbian? What would it be like if we knew he or she had a partner? Can we countenance details of intimacy that we can only imagine and that we would personally find distasteful? How would we *feel* about all that?

The truth is that we have no business imagining the details of intimacy of the lives of *any* other people, whatever their sexual orientation. The intimate details of the lives of others are only a matter of public interest if they make them so—for instance, if one of them abuses or injures the other, so that outside intervention is requested or required, or if they practise some kind of exhibitionist behaviour that shocks and scandalizes their neighbours. What they do in private is otherwise a private matter and not a proper subject for imaginative speculation.

And there is no need to imagine what it would be like to receive the ministry of gay and lesbian people, because many of them are ordained right now and some of them secretly have

---

67   See Donald Meen, "What Science is Saying," in *Hearing Diverse Voices, Seeking Common Ground*, Anglican Book Centre, 1994, p. 32, "In the end, what really distinguishes all lesbian/gay from heterosexual people is not lifestyle, but the sex of the person with whom they fall in love."

partners. Most of them minister with devotion, conviction, and commitment, while a few of them are probably as incompetent as a few heterosexuals. The healthy-minded majority of them (like the majority of the rest of the population) will wish to keep their private lives private even when their relationships are no longer condemned to be secret, furtive, and anxious.

Can we expect the whole Anglican Communion to change its traditional understanding of sexual relationships soon and unanimously? No, we cannot. People whose attitudes are shaped by a culturally imposed acceptance of prohibitions are simply not able to change easily and quickly, because it is the very framework of their universe that is at stake. People with such attitudes may not necessarily belong to tribally organized societies. The development of human cultures does not involve ceasing to belong to one kind of culture and joining another, like changing a shirt. Cultural evolution is more like the growth of a tree in successive concentric rings. We all have a tribal core, which sometimes appears in unexpected forms. Narrow and aggressive nationalism, and passionate and symbolic identification with athletic teams, are cases in point, both with a terrifyingly violent potential. So is the attraction of cult-movements, which provide a secure and sacred environment protected from a hostile world under the leadership of a charismatic elder. So is the conviction that certain human phenomena (like homosexuality) are absolutely wrong, *because everyone knows that this has always been the case*. It is possible that tribal assumptions may have had their origin in practices that were supposed to foster health (like circumcision, or not eating pork), or in social organization that protected family alignments and prevented explosive outbreaks of sexually motivated rage (like the obligation of all members of the tribe to procreate, or the preservation of male property rights over females). However, as signs of tribal identity, such residual assumptions persist long after the conditions of their origins may have changed or vanished. Tribal cultures are conservative and do not ask, "Why?"

Tribal culture is concerned with survival, and survival of the tribe first of all. With the emergence of the culture of the towns there is a shift from survival as perdurance to survival in meaningful and ordered ways. The individual begins to assume more importance. Questions of responsibility begin to be more central than ritual correctness. We can see this happening in the writings of the prophets Jeremiah and Ezekiel, both of whom challenge a principle laid down in the second of the ten commandments: that God would punish children for the iniquity of parents to the third and fourth generation, and would show steadfast love to the thousandth generation of those who love and obey God. Jeremiah looks forward to a new era in which people would no longer recite the proverb, "The parents have eaten sour grapes, and the children's teeth are set on edge." People will be punished for their own sin, says Jeremiah; those who have eaten sour grapes will themselves shudder.[68] The primacy of the tribe as a collective was giving way to the emergence of a community of individuals who have to take responsibility for their own actions. We have already looked at the writings of Amos, Micah, and the author of the final part of the book of Isaiah, and their attack on liturgy and fasting when they are given priority over justice and compassion. We witness in their thought the beginnings of a transition from tribal ritual and taboo to the possibility of a better-ordered society.

---

68   Jeremiah 31.29–30, Ezekiel 18.1–4. Compare Exodus 20.5, Deuteronomy 5.9, and Numbers 14.18.

The culture of the towns did not abolish tribal instincts, but it absorbed and transcended them. The historic event of the ministry of Jesus may be set in the process of this transition. He followed Jeremiah, Ezekiel, the author of the final part of Isaiah, and other prophets in looking for the law behind the law, the law of the heart, the kingdom where the goal of the law is realized in humility, simplicity, and freedom.

After the time of Jesus and the subsequent destruction of Jerusalem, the Jewish religious tradition went in two directions. Jewish scholars developed their legal heritage into a vast system of interpretation that eventually became the Talmud. Christian leaders followed Paul's theology of grace instead of law, but they also accepted his practical advice for the ordering of the Christian community as binding, and eventually established a firm system of discipline that looked an awful lot like law. By the fourth century the expectations laid on would-be converts were so severe that many (including the emperor Constantine) delayed their baptism until their deathbed.

Meanwhile, the culture of the towns was producing a civilization built on the ideals of reason, order, and law. Certain things are required or prohibited, so that the life of the community may be harmonious and provide an environment hospitable to prosperity and peace. Of course, the history of Western society is not without its barbarisms in the form of unjust laws and brutal rulers, but the ideal is there, fed by the heritage of Greek philosophy and Roman law. The church became a full-time partner in this process, especially in the period after the disruption of civilization by tribal invasions from the east. The church eventually contributed a towering system of law that regulated many aspects of social life beyond the concerns of piety. When the central authority of the church collapsed in much of northern Europe in the sixteenth century, the Bible, ostensibly a symbol of freedom, became in many places a lawbook. By this time, Paul's unquestioning acceptance of an ancient tribal rejection of homosexuality as a social norm[69] had become the basis of an inflexible regulation.

Can we expect people whose concept of morality was shaped by the long friendship of reason and law (town life people) to abandon the centuries-old tradition that homosexuality is contrary to nature and therefore perverse, and must be made illegal and punishable under law? Not all at once, perhaps, but precisely because of their tradition of rational discourse and analysis, we can at least expect them to be prepared to *discuss* the matter, to *listen* to the experience of gay men and lesbian women, to *evaluate* the philosophic assumptions on which their judgements rest, to attempt to think dispassionately about issues whose discussion often owes more to emotion than to reason, to recognize the frightful brutality to which homosexual people have been subjected when their society has effectively treated them as outside the law,[70] to listen to psychiatrists who have removed homosexuality from their lists of disorders. Many people who have followed a regime like this have changed their minds already.

However, for those of us who find ourselves called or compelled to be Christians in a post-modern, secular age, the questions are different. Insofar as we are still held in the grip of unconsidered tribal assumptions, we want to be rid of them. And we are suspicious of law—not of harmony and order but of law as a means of improvement. Many laws are memorials to

---

69 Romans 1.26f. Actually, Paul treats homosexuality as a consequence of idolatry. He may have had a particular cult in mind.

70 I write a few days after the death of Matthew Shepard, a young gay man who was pistol-whipped and left for dead, tied to a fence like a crucified scarecrow, near Laramie, Wyoming.

failure—a necessary corrective, but nevertheless a tribute to the injustice, indifference, and exploitation that led to their adoption. Law is often merely a way to prevent things from getting worse; it only occasionally makes them better, and it seldom achieves that generosity of spirit that is a component of holiness. Law may provide us with a list of concerns, but it is not the road to transfiguration. We are suspicious of great theories that tell us exactly where everyone fits—marriage here, contracts there, this duty and that duty in their places, and the people who don't fit, nowhere. And, strangely, we feel deep down that the gospel of Jesus speaks with great affinity to this post-modern culture!

A major element in Jesus' proclamation was what he called, "the kingdom of God." It was a state of being in which the ordinary values and power structures of human society were reversed in favour of an open mutuality that had the potential for inner renewal and social change. He seems to have demonstrated this message by identification with those whom the respectable levels of his society avoided and belittled, and by carrying that identification to the point of physical contact and companionship at table. He made few if any demands, apparently expecting a tangible experience of the kingdom to exert its own effect on those who followed him. He did, it is true, call people to repent—but the word in Greek does not carry the guilt-ridden, self-inflicted moral agony that later generations of Christians attached to it: it means simply, "turn around," as one might turn from gazing at dark storm clouds to discover a rainbow in the opposite sky. He did, it is true, tell the woman taken in adultery to "sin no more," but it was sound advice in a context where adultery was a capital offence (as she knew only too well). In any case, he did not scold her.

The truth is that Jesus said very little about sexuality and sexual sins. His remarks on lustful looking[71] may have been directed against those who congratulated themselves because they had not *actually* committed adultery (presumably despising those who had), but failed to realize that desire and intent were the real issues. Matthew and Mark both quote Jesus' reference to his generation as "adulterous," but his words may have been an echo of the prophets' use of adultery as a metaphor for faithlessness, especially the infidelity of idolatry.[72]

In any case, Jesus seems to have been more exercised by sins like hypocrisy, self-righteousness, and the delusion that one could achieve true holiness by skating cleverly through a technically correct observance of a moral code. He appears to have been much more distressed by claims to be holier than someone else,[73] by public arrogance (especially on the part of those who exploited others),[74] and by conspicuous displays of religiosity and piety.[75] Jesus' care for those who were rejected and oppressed suggests that the sins with which he was most concerned were the rejection and oppression of others. It is noteworthy that when a rich young man assured Jesus that he had kept a specified

71 Matthew 5.27–28
72 See Jeremiah 3.6–9, where Israel is accused of "committing adultery with stone and tree," and Ezekiel 23.36–39. The issue is complicated in the prophets because idolatry often involved intercourse with prostitutes of the cult, and the prophets also used the term in its ordinary literal sense. For Hosea, the adultery of his wife finds a parallel in the faithless idolatry of Israel.
73 Luke 18.9–14.
74 Mark 12.38–40.
75 Matthew 6.1–4.

list of commandments, Jesus told him that if he wanted to be perfect, he should sell all that he had and give the money to the poor.[76] Apparently *keeping the commandments had not made him perfect*. As far as we know, Jesus said not one word about homosexuality.

The question is not whether there is a place in the kingdom of God for homosexual people who love one another and are committed to living together. The question is whether there is a place in God's kingdom for the rest of us if we insist on investing a few passages of Scripture with an importance we do not attach to many others, in order to condemn them. The question is whether there is a place for *us* in God's kingdom if we claim an authority for the Bible that goes far beyond our own established tradition and that the Bible does not claim for itself, in order to prohibit homosexual people who live in faithful and committed loving relationships from exercising a ministry in the church. Jesus was prepared to reverse one of the ten commandments, relax another, and challenge the Mosaic law on divorce in the interests of love, freedom, and responsibility among his followers. What are the implications of this action for our interpretation of the biblical references to homosexuality? What are the implications of this action for us? Does Lambeth 1998 Resolution I.10 truly reflect the kingdom of God?

Our primary symbol of God's kingdom is Jesus himself, the man who is God but still man, the "window into God at work," as John Robinson called him,[77] the one who "reveals God by being utterly transparent to him [sic], precisely as he is nothing in

---

76   Matthew 19.16–22.
77   J.A.T. Robinson, *Honest to God*, SCM Press Ltd., London, 1963, p. 71.

himself."[78] In his teaching, caring, living, dying, conquering, we see what God (and God's reign) is like. Our secondary symbols are the bath of new birth, the table where we are accepted in and through one another in the act of remembering Jesus, and the collection of stories, wisdom, hymns, teaching, and insight that we call the "word of God." Through this record we participate actively in the liberation, challenge, new vision, and new life that is God's kingdom unfolding in time and space.

The pilgrimage that the Bible describes is not something that happened long ago that we have to swallow like other historical data; the Bible is a *living* symbol that enables us to participate in that pilgrimage right now. And this means we must engage with it, and press back where we find that one part of the tradition may not mesh with the trajectory of the whole —just as Amos, and Micah, and Jeremiah, and Ezekiel, and the author of the final part of the book Isaiah, and Jesus himself pressed back on the tradition. Just as Christians who opposed slavery, the prohibition of usury, and the subjugation of women pressed back on the tradition. This engagement with the tradition is what the gift of the Holy Spirit is about: it is searching for the spirit of the tradition, rather than the letter, in our own day.

It is in this spirit and in this light that we must now review and evaluate the attitudes and disciplines our church has inherited in regard to homosexuality. As a church, a collection of fallible, opinionated, often sinful people, joined only in our desire (however weak) to follow Jesus, we, too, are a symbol. These people (us) are God's kingdom, but are still these people (us). When

---

78   Ibid., p. 73.

the church claims to be God's kingdom and forgets it is still people like us, it becomes not only a self-worshipping idol but a monster. On the other hand, when it ceases to struggle to see the kingdom within the tattered folds of its own ranks here and now, it loses its role as symbol altogether. It floats away on a cloud of angelism, or provides a front of respectability for an unjust society. We can only begin to see ourselves as kingdom if we start and finish with the people we are.

It is not enough to assure homosexual people, that "they are loved by God and that all baptized, believing and faithful persons, regardless of sexual orientation, are full members of the Body of Christ," while rejecting the only way they can love each other as "incompatible with Scripture," and on such flimsy grounds as we have seen. The time has come to imagine the kingdom of God peopled with our gay and lesbian brothers and sisters, not as second-class citizens who must pretend to leave their love at the door but on that basis of acceptance with which Jesus welcomed all those whom others rejected. After all, none of us has better credentials for belonging.

Appendix 1

IN FEBRUARY 1997, eighty Anglican leaders representing provinces "of the South," that is, provinces of the Anglican Communion in non-Western cultural settings, met in Kuala Lumpur, Malaysia, for the Second Anglican Encounter in the South. The theme of their meeting was Scripture and mission. They adopted the following resolution.[79]

1. God's glory and loving purposes have been revealed in the creation of humankind. (Romans 1:18, Genesis 1:26, 27) Among the multiplicity of his gifts we are blessed with our sexuality.
2. Since the Fall (Genesis 3), life has been impaired and God's own purposes spoilt. Our fallen state has affected every sphere of our being, which includes our sexuality. Sexual deviation has existed in every time and in most cultures. Jesus' teaching about lust in the Sermon on the Mount (Mathew 5:26–30) makes it clear that sexual sin is a real danger and temptation to us all.
3. It is, therefore, with an awareness of our own vulnerability to sexual sin that we express our profound concern about recent developments relating to Church discipline and moral teaching in some provinces in the North—specifically, the ordination of practicing homosexuals and the blessing of same-sex unions.
4. While acknowledging the complexities of our sexual nature and the strong drives it places within us, we are quite clear about God's will in these areas as expressed in the Bible.

---

79 Sourced in Stephen F. Noll, *The Handwriting on the Wall: A Plea to the Anglican Communion*, Latimer Press, Solon, Ohio, 1998, pp. 45–47.

5. The Scripture bears witness to God's will regarding human sexuality which is to be expressed only within the lifelong union of a man and a woman in (holy) matrimony.
6. The Holy Scriptures are clear in teaching that all sexual promiscuity is sin. We are convinced that this includes homosexual practices, between men or women, as well as heterosexual relationships outside marriage.
7. We believe that the clear and unambiguous teaching of the Holy Scriptures about human sexuality is of great help to Christians as it provides clear boundaries.
8. We find no conflict between clear biblical teaching and sensitive pastoral care. The call to repentance precedes forgiveness and is part of the healing process. We see this in the ministry of Jesus, for example his response to the adulterous woman, "neither do I condemn you. *Go and sin no more*." (John 8:11)
9. We are deeply concerned that the setting aside of biblical teaching in such actions as the ordination of practicing homosexuals and the blessing of same-sex union calls into question the authority of the Holy Scriptures. This is totally unacceptable to us.
10. We encourage the Church to care for all those who are trapped in their sexual brokenness and to become the channel of Christ's compassion, love and healing towards them. We wish to stand alongside and welcome them into a process of being made whole and restored within our communities of faith. We would also affirm and resource those who exercise pastoral ministry in this area.
11. This leads us to express concern about mutual accountability and interdependence within our Anglican Communion. As provinces and dioceses we need to learn how to seek each other's counsel and wisdom in the spirit of true unity, and to reach a common mind, before embarking on radical changes to Church discipline and moral teaching.
12. We live in a global village and must be more aware that the way we act in one part of the world can radically affect the mission and witness of the Church in another.

Appendix 2

ARE YOU PERSUADED that the Holy Scriptures contain sufficiently all doctrine required of necessity for eternal salvation through faith in Jesus Christ? and are you determined, out of the said Scriptures to instruct the people committed to your charge, and to teach nothing, as required of necessity to eternal salvation, but that which you shall be persuaded may be concluded and proved by the Scriptures? *Book of Common Prayer, 1662, The Ordering of Priests.*

Are you persuaded that the Holy Scriptures contain sufficiently all doctrine required of necessity for eternal salvation through faith in Jesus Christ? And are you determined, out of the same Holy Scriptures to instruct the people committed to your charge; and to teach or maintain nothing, as required of necessity to eternal salvation, but that which you shall be persuaded may be concluded and proved by the same? *Book of Common Prayer, 1662, The Consecration of Bishops.*

Appendix 3

FROM THE THIRTY-NINE ARTICLES

VI. *Of the Sufficiency of the holy Scriptures for salvation.*

Holy Scripture containeth all things necessary to salvation: so that whatsoever is not read therein, nor may be proved thereby, is not to be required of any man, that it should be believed as an article of the Faith, or be thought requisite or necessary to salvation. In the name of the holy Scripture we do understand those Canonical Books of the Old and New Testament, of whose authority was never any doubt in the Church.

Of the Names and Number of the Canonical Books.

Genesis,
Exodus,
Leviticus,
Numbers,
Deuteronomy,
Joshua,
Judges,
Ruth,
The First Book of Samuel,
The Second Book of Samuel,
The First Book of Kings,
The Second Book of Kings,
The First Book of Chronicles,
The Second Book of Chronicles,
The First Book of Esdras [Ezra],
The Second Book of Esdras [Nehemiah],
The Book of Esther,
The Book of Job,
The Psalms,
The Proverbs,
Ecclesiastes or Preacher,
Cantica, or Songs of Solomon,
Four Prophets the greater,
Twelve Prophets the less.

And the other Books (as *Hierome* saith) the Church doth read for example of life and instruction of manners; but yet doth it not apply them to establish any doctrine; such are these following:

The Third Book of Esdras [I Esdras],
The Fourth Book of Esdras [II Esdras],
The Book of Tobias,
The Book of Judith,
The rest of the Book of Esther,
The Book of Wisdom,
Jesus the Son of Sirach [or Ecclesiasticus],
Baruch the Prophet,
The Song of the Three Children,
The Story of Susanna,
Of Bel and the Dragon,
The Prayer of Manasses,
The First Book of Maccabees,
The Second Book of Maccabees.

All the Books of the New Testament, as they are common received, we do receive, and account them Canonical.

VII. *Of the Old Testament.*

The Old Testament is not contrary to the New: for both in the Old and New Testament everlasting life is offered to Mankind by Christ, who is the only Mediator between God and Man, being both God and Man. Wherefore they are not to be heard, which feign that the old Fathers did look only for transitory promises. Although the Law given from God by Moses, as touching Ceremonies and Rites, do not bind Christian men, nor the Civil precepts thereof ought of necessity to be received in any commonwealth; yet notwithstanding, no Christian man whatsoever is free from the obedience of the Commandments which are called Moral.

XX. *Of the Authority of the Church.*

The Church hath power to decree Rites or Ceremonies, and authority in Controversies of Faith: And yet it is not lawful for the Church to ordain any thing that is contrary to God's Word written, neither may it so expound one place of Scripture, that it be repugnant to another. Wherefore, although the Church be a witness and a keeper of holy Writ, yet, as it ought not to decree any thing against the same, so besides the same ought it not to enforce any thing to be believed for necessity of Salvation.